Glorifying God

through the

Psalms

A DEVOTIONAL

I will give thanks to You,
Lord my God, with all my heart,
And I will glorify Your name forever.
Psalm 86:12

David and Cynthia Lanius

Glorifying God through the Psalms
by David and Cynthia Lanius

ISBN 978-1-7355648-3-8

Printed in the United States of America

Cover art https://shotstash.com/license/

DEDICATION

To our family,

Our children: Ben and Valerie, who have honored us beyond measure, and the two, Rachel and Stacey, they found for us to love as our own,

Our grandchildren: Andrew, Eli, Nate, Hannah, Jacob, Zach, and Anna Grace, who are the crown of the aged,

Our brothers and sisters: Buddy, Charlotte, Don, Cindy, Tommy, Kay, Kim, Mark, Jamie, Rob, and their families,

And our spiritual children, grandchildren, brothers, and sisters in the Lord,

We lovingly dedicate this book.

The Lord will protect you from all evil;
He will keep your soul.
The Lord will guard your going out and your coming in
From this time forth and forever.
Psalm 121:7-8

CONTENTS

INTRODUCTION

O send out Your light and Your truth, let them lead me;
Let them bring me to Your holy hill
And to Your dwelling places.
Psalm 43:3

There must be hundreds of books about the Psalms, so why another one? Rather than a book that seeks to explain the Psalms in detail, this one is designed to engage us in the worship of God using the Psalms as a model. To provide flexibility for personal or class use, it is organized around fifty-two topics composing thirteen lessons.

Why Psalms? No book of the sacred writings devotes itself more fully to the appreciation of our Holy Father. Even though the Psalms were originally sung, and the melodies have been lost, the beauty and power of the words draw us near to God. The Psalms remind us over and over of His deep love for us, as in Psalm 36:7: "How precious is Your lovingkindness, O God!"

Do we yearn to worship the Lord more in our daily lives? Notice the fervor of David. In Psalm 63:1, he says, "O God, You are my God; I shall seek You earnestly; My soul thirsts for You, my flesh yearns for You, In a dry and weary land where there is no water."

Do we long to delight in Him and in His word? Psalm 1:2 speaks of the blessed man: "But his delight is in the law of the Lord, And in His law he meditates day and night." Likewise, is our request of the Lord, "Open my eyes, that I may behold wonderful things from Your law" (Psalm 119:18)?

As we begin, let us notice the word "selah," a musical term which is thought to mean "to pause." Found 71 times in Psalms, selah asks us to pause, so we can meditate for a moment on the text. So when you see it, pause and reflect, as in Psalm 24:10: "Who

1

is this King of glory? The LORD of hosts, He is the King of glory. *Selah.*" That is something great upon which to meditate.

A word on words: many of the words that we will discuss vary from translation to translation. For example,

Psalm 6:4
Turn, LORD, and deliver me; save me because of your unfailing love (NIV).
Return, O LORD, deliver my soul: oh save me for thy mercies' sake (KJV).
Return, O LORD, rescue my soul; Save me because of Your lovingkindness (NASB1995).

1)"Unfailing love" 2) "mercies' sake" and 3) "lovingkindness" are all translated interchangeably. This study relies heavily on words, and this verse could be used in either one of the lessons on these three topics, so we made some arbitrary decisions about where to put them. Also, be aware that we are primarily using the New American Standard Bible, 1995.

As we begin, let this be our prayer,

Every day I will bless You,
And I will praise Your name forever and ever.
Psalm 145:2

LESSON I

O Worship the King

NOTES

1

Praise the Lord

For the LORD is a great God And a great King above all gods,
⁴In whose hand are the depths of the earth, The peaks of the
mountains are His also. ⁵The sea is His, for it was He who made it,
And His hands formed the dry land. ⁶Come, let us worship and bow
down, Let us kneel before the LORD our Maker.
Psalm 95:3-6

"For the Lord is a great God." What joy fills our hearts with those words. "Come, let us worship and bow down, Let us kneel before the LORD our Maker." No matter what we are doing today, our day will be blessed by reading those words. Let us read them with our whole hearts. Try reading them out loud so that we can hear them and impress our hearts with them.

Psalms is a book of praise. The word praise is found 147 times in Psalms (NASB1995), not even counting all its synonyms. The Psalmists praised God, and so do we, because He is worthy of it. "Great is the Lord, and highly to be praised, And His greatness is unsearchable" (Psalm 145:3). KJV says "greatly to be praised." Not only is God great, but our praise of Him should be great. No words of praise could be too great to praise the LORD. We should not be sparing with our praise. Instead, make it great.

"And His greatness is unsearchable." When we meditate most on His greatness and search His nature most thoughtfully, we will still find ourselves surrounded with wonders too great to behold. In Psalm 139:1, David says that the Lord has searched him and knows everything about him. But we cannot say that we know everything about God. His greatness is too great for finite man to comprehend. In Ephesians 3:8, the apostle Paul talked of the "unfathomable riches of Christ."

Praising God to others is a way to let our lights shine. Acts 2:47 says that all those who had believed were "praising God and having favor with all the people. And the Lord was adding to their number day by day those who were being saved." We have heard this verse maybe hundreds of times, but because it tells us how we get into the church, we focus on the last part of the verse. But quoting again, the believers were "praising God and having favor with all the people." The early church praised God, and it had a favorable impact on the people that heard it.

Can we use this study to improve and increase our praise, making it greater? Praise can become a habit: waking up in praise, spending the day in praise, and going to sleep in praise. Let us take an opportunity to praise God to someone new. But we cannot praise God to others out of one side of our mouths and speak evil out of the other side (James 3:10).

Suggestions for further study: Do a word search for "praise," either in an online Bible or a concordance, and make a list of praises to read every day. Read praises with others. Let us be careful to honor God with our hearts as well as our lips (Matthew 15:8).

Daily Praises

Psalm 18:3 I call upon the LORD, who is worthy to be praised, And I am saved from my enemies.
Psalm 34:1 I will bless the LORD at all times; His praise shall continually be in my mouth.
Psalm 40:3 He put a new song in my mouth, a song of praise to our God; Many will see and fear And will trust in the LORD.
Psalm 48:1 Great is the LORD, and greatly to be praised In the city of our God, His holy mountain.
Psalm 51:15 O Lord, open my lips, That my mouth may declare Your praise.
Psalm 63:3 Because Your lovingkindness is better than life, My lips will praise You.
Psalm 67:3 Let the peoples praise You, O God; Let all the peoples praise You.
Psalm 104:34 Let my meditation be pleasing to Him; As for me, I shall be glad in the LORD.

2

Thanks Be to God

I will give thanks to the LORD according to His righteousness
And will sing praise to the name of the LORD Most High.
Psalm 7:17

Thanksgiving is intertwined with praise in the Psalms. In fact, the main Hebrew word for thanks, "yadah," is defined in Strong's Concordance as "to give thanks, laud or praise, in ritual, public or personal praise." It is found mostly in the book of Psalms, some 70 times.

One description of this word is "acknowledging what is right about God in praise and thanksgiving." Consider these examples: "Give thanks to the LORD, for He is good; For His lovingkindness is everlasting" (Psalm 118:1), and "Enter His gates with thanksgiving And His courts with praise. Give thanks to Him, bless His name. ⁵For the Lord is good; His lovingkindness is everlasting And His faithfulness to all generations" (Psalm 100:4-5). I thank you, Oh Lord, for You are good. That is how the Psalmists say to give thanks.

God wants us to feel and express gratitude because it is good for us. We teach our children to say "thank you" so they can learn gratitude. God wants us to learn to be thankful for all His gifts, not because He needs gratitude, but because we need to express it. We must remember that He is the source of all good. Thankfulness keeps our hearts in a right relationship with the Giver of all good gifts. It reminds us that God is not an accessory; He is our all in all.

Our greatest gifts are our spiritual blessings in Christ and we should express gratitude for them often:

Romans 6:17 But thanks be to God that though you were slaves of sin, you became obedient from the heart to that form of teaching to which you were committed.

Romans 7:24-25a Wretched man that I am! Who will set me free from the body of this death? [25]Thanks be to God through Jesus Christ our Lord!

1 Corinthians 15:57 But thanks be to God, who gives us the victory through our Lord Jesus Christ.

2 Corinthians 4:15 For all things are for your sakes, so that the grace which is spreading to more and more people may cause the giving of thanks to abound to the glory of God.

2 Corinthians 9:15 Thanks be to God for His indescribable gift!

Over and over, the Psalmists show us what it means to be thankful to God even in times of fear, sadness, and grief. Gratitude draws our eyes away from ourselves and helps us focus on the goodness of God and our dependence on Him.

Suggestions for further study: Do a word search for "thanks" and study all the references. Think more about giving thanks to God for who He is and what He does. Keep a written prayer list or prayer journal that includes God's attributes and spiritual blessings.

Daily Thanksgiving

Psalm 35:18 I will give You thanks in the great congregation; I will praise You among a mighty throng.

Psalm 105:1 Oh give thanks to the LORD, call upon His name; Make known His deeds among the peoples.

Psalm 119:62 At midnight I shall rise to give thanks to You Because of Your righteous ordinances.

Psalm 136:1-3 Give thanks to the LORD, for He is good, For His lovingkindness is everlasting. Give thanks to the God of gods, For His lovingkindness is everlasting. Give thanks to the Lord of lords, For His lovingkindness is everlasting.

Psalm 138:2 I will bow down toward Your holy temple And give thanks to Your name for Your lovingkindness and Your truth; For You have magnified Your word according to all Your name.

3

For to You I Pray

O God, You are my God; I shall seek You earnestly;
My soul thirsts for You, my flesh yearns for You, In a dry and
weary land where there is no water. [2]Thus I have seen You in the
sanctuary, To see Your power and Your glory. [3]Because Your
lovingkindness is better than life, My lips will praise You.
[4]So I will bless You as long as I live; I will lift up my hands in Your
name. [5]My soul is satisfied as with marrow and fatness,
And my mouth offers praises with joyful lips.
Psalm 63:1-5

What a powerful, yet tender prayer David prays. It seems clear
that this was something that he did deeply and often. Like praise
and thanksgiving, prayer is an integral part of the Psalms and is also
an integral part of a Christian's life.

Who is your friend with whom conversation is so satisfying that
you could talk for hours? It is hard for us to understand why our
prayers may not be as satisfying. What a great blessing this
communion with God is. He will listen. Isn't it amazing that the
great Lord and King of the universe will commune with us?

Preachers often admonish us to pray more. Maybe that is not
the primary problem. Maybe we first need to pray differently. It can
take many years to learn to pray from the heart. We may pray more
formal prayers like we hear in the church, or we may pray
memorized prayers without giving them too much thought. Our
prayers can be intimate conversation with the Father, tender
yearnings that we share only with Him. They can be sorrows for our
weaknesses and longings for strength. They can be joyous
expressions of what we hold dearest. Or they can be confessions of
our greatest temptations. Our confessions will not shock God. He
knows us better than we know ourselves. "O God, it is You who

knows my folly, And my wrongs are not hidden from You" (Psalm 69:5).

When we are weak or strong, we need to pray. Let us say it: "I need to pray." We do not pray only in order to check it off a list of things we are supposed to do. Our hearts should yearn to talk to God. And when we do not feel that yearning, we must pray anyway. It could go something like this, "Lord, my heart is weak. You know that I do not feel as I should about praying to You. Forgive me, Lord. Take away my self-sufficiency and my busyness. Help me pray as I should." Again, Psalm 69:5 says, "O God, it is You who knows my folly, And my wrongs are not hidden from You."

Suggestions for further study: Make a list of your reasons to pray. I want to talk to God about_____ because _____.

Daily Prayers

Psalm 5:2-3 Heed the sound of my cry for help, my King and my God, For to You I pray. In the morning, O LORD, You will hear my voice; In the morning I will order my prayer to You and eagerly watch.

Psalm 25:1-7 To You, O LORD, I lift up my soul. [2] O my God, in You I trust, Do not let me be ashamed; Do not let my enemies exult over me. [3] Indeed, none of those who wait for You will be ashamed; Those who deal treacherously without cause will be ashamed. [4] Make me know Your ways, O LORD; Teach me Your paths. [5] Lead me in Your truth and teach me, For You are the God of my salvation; For You I wait all the day. [6] Remember, O LORD, Your compassion and Your lovingkindnesses, For they have been from of old. [7] Do not remember the sins of my youth or my transgressions; According to Your lovingkindness remember me, For Your goodness' sake, O LORD.

Psalm 66:19-20 But certainly God has heard; He has given heed to the voice of my prayer. [20] Blessed be God, Who has not turned away my prayer Nor His lovingkindness from me.

Psalm 86:6-7 Give ear, O Lord, to my prayer; And give heed to the voice of my supplications! [7] In the day of my trouble I shall call upon You, For You will answer me.

4

Sing for Joy

Sing to the LORD a new song; Sing to the LORD, all the earth.
²Sing to the LORD, bless His name.
Psalm 96:1-2

Because the Psalms was the hymnbook of the Israelites, it is, as we would expect, full of references to singing. We read most of the Psalms today, except for the few that have been set to music, so we sometimes forget that back then, these were songs that would have been sung, perhaps in chant. Praise, thanksgiving, prayers, and singing praises are great joys for the Christian, and wonderful gifts from God. Let us thank God for singing.

Can anything touch our hearts more than singing praises? Do we find times in the day to sing praises to God at least in our hearts? In the car? As we exercise? As we do chores? We can even sing in our hearts in public places. I remember so vividly my sisters as girls every night in the kitchen doing the dishes singing hymns together.

Have you ever heard someone say, "Oh, I can't sing," meaning it doesn't sound good? If we sing from the heart, God hears us in perfect pitch. Yes, no matter what we sound like to man, we can sound beautiful to God. And we should hear each other like God hears us. Listen to someone singing like a bullfrog and hear him or her like God hears. Make your heart hear its beauty. If you think you sound like a bullfrog, remember, God loves it, so you love it! I Samuel 16:7 says, "God sees not as man sees, for man looks at the outward appearance, but the LORD looks at the heart." He hears that way too.

Sometimes we hear Christians say, "I don't like to sing." So, why not? We should be aware that we are pouring our hearts out, "speaking to one another," and "making melody with your heart to the Lord" (Ephesians 5:19). It is like saying "I don't like to pray." Are we just too lazy to sing? Is it easier to just sit there and listen? God gave us singing because He knows it is good for us. We must work on our attitude if this is a problem for us.

Singing is a combination of words and music that can stir us to deep emotion unlike just hearing words spoken. Let us strive to make our singing mean more to us as we seek God through singing. Through praise, thanksgiving, prayer, and song, we worship the King, the greatest privilege that God bestows on man.

Suggestions for further study: Make a list of songs that touch your heart in some way. Then, make another list of songs that you can sing a verse or two without a book and sing! We need to sing, so let us sing. Next time your family sits down to watch TV, first sing a hymn together.

Daily Singing

Psalm 33:1 Sing for joy in the LORD, O you righteous ones; Praise is becoming to the upright.
Psalm 47:7 For God is the King of all the earth; Sing praises with a skillful psalm.
Psalm 59:16 But as for me, I shall sing of Your strength; Yes, I shall joyfully sing of Your lovingkindness in the morning, For You have been my stronghold And a refuge in the day of my distress.
Psalm 66:2 Sing the glory of His name; Make His praise glorious.
Psalm 95:1-6 O come, let us sing for joy to the LORD, Let us shout joyfully to the rock of our salvation. ²Let us come before His presence with thanksgiving, Let us shout joyfully to Him with psalms. ³For the LORD is a great God And a great King above all gods, ⁴In whose hand are the depths of the earth, The peaks of the mountains are His also. ⁵ The sea is His, for it was He who made it, And His hands formed the dry land. ⁶Come, let us worship and bow down, Let us kneel before the LORD our Maker.
Psalm 108:1 My heart is steadfast, O God; I will sing, I will sing praises, even with my soul.
Psalm 119:172 Let my tongue sing of Your word, For all Your commandments are righteousness.

LESSON II

In His Time

NOTES

5

Trust in the Lord

It is better to take refuge in the LORD Than to trust in man. It is
better to take refuge in the LORD Than to trust in princes.
Psalm 118:8-9

A common refrain for David is that He trusts in the Lord and
in His word. Strong's defines trust (982) here as "to have
confidence, be confident, to be bold, to be secure." Trust removes
fear. His trust in God allows David to say, "What can mere man do
to me?" (Psalm 56:4, 11; 118:6). The Hebrew writer also
emphasized this in Hebrews 13:6, quoting the Psalm: "So that we
confidently say, 'The Lord is my helper, I will not be afraid. What
will man do to me?'"

Our focus verse above says, "It is better to take refuge in the
LORD Than to trust in man." People are not always trustworthy,
but we can trust God. The Lord God Almighty is completely
trustworthy. Do we take His trustworthiness for granted? It is no
small thing. *I* will fall. *I* will stumble. But God will not. Many, many
times we abuse God's love by unfaithfulness. Our sin grieves Him,
but He is always willing and eager to take us back. We can trust
that.

It is not enough to say we trust in God. We must act on that
trust. "In God we trust" is the official motto of the United States,
and yet no one could say that America's government relies on God.

Trusting God does not mean a trouble-free life. Joseph, for
instance, trusted in God, refusing to sin with Potiphar's wife, yet he
was wrongly accused of rape and spent years in prison. Trusting
God means that no matter what happens, we will turn *to* Him rather
than *away* from Him. We may have troubles, but we will rely on
Him and His word.

Too often the temptation is to trust self rather than God — I know what is important, what I think, what I want, what I need. But Proverbs 3:5 nips that thinking in the bud. "Trust in the LORD with all your heart And do not lean on your own understanding." We can trust in Him, have confidence in Him, and thank Him for His trustworthiness and faithfulness. The Psalmist did: "The Lord is my strength and my shield; My heart trusts in Him, and I am helped; Therefore my heart exults, And with my song I shall thank Him" (Psalm 28:7).

Suggestions for further study: Think of others in the scriptures who clearly trusted God in adversity. We talked about Joseph's trust. What about Abraham's? Daniel's? Make a list of hymns that relate to trusting God. Thought question: How would trusting God more change our lives? Pray to God for more trust in Him.

Daily Trust

Psalm 26:1 Vindicate me, O LORD, for I have walked in my integrity, And I have trusted in the LORD without wavering.
Psalm 27:1 The LORD is my light and my salvation; Whom shall I fear? The LORD is the defense of my life; Whom should I dread?
Psalm 28:7 The LORD is my strength and my shield; My heart trusts in Him, and I am helped; Therefore my heart exults, And with my song I shall thank Him.
Psalm 37:5 Commit your way to the LORD, Trust also in Him, and He will do it.
Psalm 40:4 How blessed is the man who has made the LORD his trust, And has not turned to the proud, nor to those who lapse into falsehood.
Psalm 84:12 O LORD of hosts, How blessed is the man who trusts in You!
Psalm 91:2 I will say to the LORD, "My refuge and my fortress, My God, in whom I trust!"
Psalm 115:11 You who fear the LORD, trust in the LORD; He is their help and their shield.
Psalm 125:1 Those who trust in the LORD Are as Mount Zion, which cannot be moved but abides forever.

6

Hope in God

For You are my hope; O Lord GOD,
You are my confidence from my youth.
Psalm 71:5

When the Psalmist says, "For You are my hope, O Lord GOD," he is not saying, "I hope to go to heaven," although it may include that. But when the Psalmist says, "For You are my hope, O Lord GOD," he identifies God as the basis for his hope in everything in life. The same thought is in 1Timothy 4:10: "For it is for this we labor and strive, because we have fixed our hope on the living God, who is the Savior of all men, especially of believers." Trust and hope are closely related. Because we trust in God and in everything He is, everything He says, and everything He does, we can put our hope in Him.

Three times in Psalms 42 and 43, the Psalmist gives the remedy for a downcast soul. "Why are you in despair, O my soul? And why have you become disturbed within me? Hope in God, for I shall again praise Him For the help of His presence." What if your life is a mess? What if you have anxiety? What can you do? Put your hope in God and praise Him.

That is God's prescription for a satisfying life. Remember His unfailing love. He loves us at our most loathsome. Hope in His unfailing love. Hope in Him, and He will help us. Every day, find joy in hope. Romans 12:12 says that we should be "rejoicing in hope, persevering in tribulation, devoted to prayer."

Let us ask ourselves the question: Do we have a weak hope because of a weak trust in God? Whatever our circumstances, God will fill us with all joy and peace if we trust in Him. "Now may the God of hope fill you with all joy and peace in believing, so that you will abound in hope by the power of the Holy Spirit" (Romans 15:13). We can have complete hope in that. This hope connects faith and trust. Then we can say, "I believe Him; I trust Him; therefore I hope in Him." Without God, we have no hope for a good life, either here or for eternity.

Suggestions for further study: Look up the definition of "hope." How is it different from trust? Make a list of hymns that relate to hope in God. Thought question: Consider how your faith and hope may be weaker than it could be. Pray to God for more trust and hope in Him.

Daily Hope

Psalm 31:24 Be strong and let your heart take courage, All you who hope in the LORD.
Psalm 33:18 Behold, the eye of the LORD is on those who fear Him, On those who hope for His lovingkindness.
Psalm 38:15 For I hope in You, O LORD; You will answer, O Lord my God.
Psalm 39:7 And now, Lord, for what do I wait? My hope is in You.
Psalm 42:5 Why are you in despair, O my soul? And why have you become disturbed within me? Hope in God, for I shall again praise Him For the help of His presence.
Psalm 62:5 My soul, wait in silence for God only, For my hope is from Him.
Psalm 71:14 But as for me, I will hope continually, And will praise You yet more and more.
Psalm 130:7 O Israel, hope in the LORD; For with the LORD there is lovingkindness, And with Him is abundant redemption.
Psalm 131:3 O Israel, hope in the LORD From this time forth and forever.

7

Wait for the Lord

Wait for the LORD; Be strong and let your heart take courage;
Yes, wait for the LORD.
Psalm 27:14

In the last section we studied hope and before that trust. We trust in God, so we hope in Him. Now we add another link in that chain—waiting for the Lord. If we trust in Him, we will put our hope in Him. And because we hope in Him, we will not give up on Him, but we will wait for Him to do His will.

Examining the various translations reveals that waiting and hope are related. Both words are sometimes translated interchangeably. Psalm 119:43 is one example of many --in the NKJV: "And take not the word of truth utterly out of my mouth, For I have **hoped** in Your ordinances."
---In the NASB: "And do not take the word of truth utterly out of my mouth, For I **wait** for Your ordinances."

Psalm 130:5-6 says, "I wait for the LORD, my soul does wait, And in His word do I hope. ⁶My soul waits for the Lord More than the watchmen for the morning; Indeed, more than the watchmen for the morning." Imagine the watchmen all night watching for the sun to rise, how eager they are. The Psalmist is more eager for God's blessings. The Lord is more desirable to the Psalmist than the rising of the sun is to the watchmen.

Another image is used in Psalm 52:8-9: "But as for me, I am like a green olive tree in the house of God; I **trust** in the lovingkindness of God forever and ever. I will **give You thanks** forever, because You have done it, And I will **wait** on Your name, for it is good, in the presence of Your godly ones." The Psalmist is as dependent on the lovingkindness of God as the olive tree is on the caregiver for care and sustenance. And the Psalmist trusts, gives thanks, and waits.

Waiting does not mean idleness. It does not mean, "I'll sit here and wile away the time while I wait till the Lord is ready to work." While we are waiting for the Lord, we are busy in our walk with Him. Abraham waited for the Lord and believed God's promises even though he would not experience all of them during his lifetime. Noah waited for the Lord during the many years that he was building the ark, and Joseph waited for the Lord in prison. Can you think of any other examples?

Think of all the times that we wait: at the doctor's office, in line at the store, etc. Think of the challenges of waiting. If the wait is too long, we may give up and leave. What keeps us standing in that line? Hope. When we lose hope, we no longer wait. We cannot do that with God. We cannot give up on God.

Suggestions for further study: Read Galatians 6:9 and Hebrews 10:19-25, 35-36. Consider how these relate to waiting for the Lord.

Daily Waiting

Psalm 25:5 Lead me in Your truth and teach me, For You are the God of my salvation; For You I wait all the day.
Psalm 25:21 Let integrity and uprightness preserve me, For I wait for You.
Psalm 27:14 Wait for the LORD; Be strong and let your heart take courage; Yes, wait for the LORD.
Psalm 37:34 Wait for the LORD and keep His way, And He will exalt you to inherit the land; When the wicked are cut off, you will see it.
Psalm 39:7 And now, Lord, for what do I wait? My hope is in You.
Psalm 62:5 My soul, wait in silence for God only, For my hope is from Him.
Psalm 106:13 They quickly forgot His works; They did not wait for His counsel.
Psalm 119:74 May those who fear You see me and be glad, Because I wait for Your word.

8

Rejoice in the Lord

Be glad in the LORD and rejoice, you righteous ones;
And shout for joy, all you who are upright in heart.
Psalm 32:11

Rejoicing is the end of trusting, hoping, and waiting for the Lord. Being right with God is cause for joy: joy on the part of God, of Christ, of the angels, of the church, and on the part of the one who is upright in heart.

Paul said in Philippians 4:4, "Rejoice in the Lord always; again, I will say rejoice!" He also said in Romans 12:15, "Rejoice with those who rejoice, and weep with those who weep." To resolve these two statements, we must realize that when Paul said rejoice always, he did not mean to be in a state of constant giddiness and unending exuberance. Paul's lesson is that we can rejoice over our salvation every moment of our lives! We can rejoice every moment for God loves us and cares for us. No matter what our circumstances, we can rejoice in the Lord.

Paul is not saying we should rejoice over causes for mourning. When we have cause for mourning, for instance, the death of a precious child, we will mourn over that. Remember how David mourned over the illness of his child. "David therefore inquired of God for the child; and David fasted and went and lay all night on the ground. [17]The elders of his household stood beside him in order to raise him up from the ground, but he was unwilling and would not eat food with them" (2 Samuel 12:16-17). But even in our most distraught times, we still have our salvation and the love and care of our great God. We should rejoice over that always and in all ways.

Psalm 119:14 says, "I have rejoiced in the way of Your testimonies, As much as in all riches." Think about how thrilled folks are when they come into a great amount of money. The way of God's testimonies are much better than that. Psalm 119:162 says, "I rejoice at Your word, As one who finds great spoil." Picture the image of soldiers winning the battle and gaining the spoil. When we read the word of God, it is like finding great treasure. Dwell on our true riches and rejoice! Trust, hope, wait, and rejoice in the Lord, all in His time.

Psalm 149:4: "For the LORD takes pleasure in His people; He will beautify the afflicted ones with salvation." Do we ever think about God rejoicing over us? Observe the father's emotion on the return of the son in Luke 15: 22-24: "But the father said to his slaves, 'Quickly bring out the best robe and put it on him, and put a ring on his hand and sandals on his feet; ²³and bring the fattened calf, kill it, and let us eat and celebrate; ²⁴for this son of mine was dead and has come to life again; he was lost and has been found.' And they began to celebrate." How sweet it is to think of delighting the Lord rather than grieving Him. Let us thank God that it gives Him such delight to forgive and save us.

Suggestions for further study: Find other examples of rejoicing over salvation in the scriptures. Read the words to "In His Time."

Daily Rejoicing

Psalm 2:11 Worship the LORD with reverence And rejoice with trembling.
Psalm 13:5 But I have trusted in Your lovingkindness; My heart shall rejoice in Your salvation.
Psalm 32:10-11 Many are the sorrows of the wicked, But he who trusts in the LORD, lovingkindness shall surround him. ¹¹ Be glad in the LORD and rejoice, you righteous ones; And shout for joy, all you who are upright in heart.
Psalm 33:21 For our heart rejoices in Him, Because we trust in His holy name.
Psalm 68:3 But let the righteous be glad; let them exult before God; Yes, let them rejoice with gladness.
Psalm 97:1 The LORD reigns, let the earth rejoice; Let the many islands be glad.

LESSON III

God Will Take
Care of You

NOTES

9

God Gives Comfort

Even though I walk through the valley of the shadow of death,
I fear no evil, for You are with me;
Your rod and Your staff, they comfort me.
Psalm 23:4

We have painted a rather idyllic portrait of the Psalmists. If we stopped reading this book now, we would think all they did was rejoice and praise and sing, but no, there is a lot of pain and heartache in the Psalms.

In fact, there is so much sorrow in the Psalms that a group of Psalms are categorized as the "Lament Psalms." Some that are traditionally in this category include: Psalms 44, 60, 74, 79, 80, 85, 86, and 90.

A Lament Psalm typically:
1) **Addresses God**: Psalm 44:1 says simply, "O God."
2) **Expresses sorrow:** "But for Your sake we are killed all day long; We are considered as sheep to be slaughtered" (Psalm 44:22).
3) **Petitions God for help:** "Arouse Yourself, why do You sleep, O Lord? Awake, do not reject us forever" (Psalm 44:23).
4) **Expresses trust in God**: "Through You we will push back our adversaries; Through Your name we will trample down those who rise up against us" (Psalm 44:5).
5) **Praises God:** "You are my King, O God" (Psalm 44:4).

This can be a framework for appealing to the Lord for comfort. So often when we are overcome with grief, fear, or self-doubts, words fail us. I read where a person was so distraught that she just prayed the name of Jesus over and over. Even that can bring comfort.

A verse of the song, *I Bring my Sins to Thee* (by Frances R. Havergal) captures the thought of God giving comfort when we are in this state of anguish.

> I bring my grief to Thee, The grief I cannot tell;
> No words shall needed be, Thou knowest all so well;
> I bring the sorrow laid on me, O suffering Savior, all to Thee,
> O suffering Savior, all to Thee.

To go beyond that anguish and formulate words that help us ask God for comfort, we can use the Lament Psalms as a model.

Elements of a Prayer for Comfort
Address God
Express our sorrow to Him
Ask Him for help
Express our trust in Him
Praise Him and Thank Him

Suggestions for further study: Many hymns are designed to give comfort. Make a list of hymns and sing a verse as a prayer.

Daily Comfort

Psalm 30:10-12 Hear, O LORD, and be gracious to me; O LORD, be my helper. [11]You have turned for me my mourning into dancing; You have loosed my sackcloth and girded me with gladness,[12]That my soul may sing praise to You and not be silent. O LORD my God, I will give thanks to You forever.
Psalm 32:10 Many are the sorrows of the wicked, But he who trusts in the LORD, lovingkindness shall surround him.
Psalm 86:17 Show me a sign for good, That those who hate me may see it and be ashamed, Because You, O LORD, have helped me and comforted me.
Psalm 119:50 This is my comfort in my affliction, That Your word has revived me.
Psalm 119:76 O may Your lovingkindness comfort me, According to Your word to Your servant.

10

The Lord Gives Peace

Lovingkindness and truth have met together;
Righteousness and peace have kissed each other.
Psalm 85:10

"Righteousness and peace have kissed each other." We have not really talked about the beauty of the poetic language of the Psalms, but this is a lovely example of it. The context of this verse is a prayer for mercy on the land. Righteousness of the people brought peace to the land, so in a figure, righteousness and peace kiss.

The Hebrew word translated as peace is "shalom," and according to Strong's, it means not only the absence of conflict, but it also conveys completeness, soundness, and reconciliation.

Think of peace as completeness. We often speak of peace being broken. Making peace is putting the pieces together, making things complete. When we lose our inner peace, we feel shattered. And even though peace with others, peace with nations, etc. is described in the scriptures, the true focus is peace with God.

In Isaiah 9:6, Isaiah predicted the coming of One who would bring peace to earth. "For a child will be born to us, a son will be given to us; And the government will rest on His shoulders; And His name will be called Wonderful Counselor, Mighty God, Eternal Father, Prince of Peace." Upon Jesus' birth, the angels sang, "Glory to God in the highest, And on earth peace among men with whom He is pleased" (Luke 2:14).

Sin separates us from God. "But your iniquities have made a separation between you and your God, And your sins have hidden His face from you so that He does not hear" (Isaiah 59:2). Our relationship is broken, but Jesus makes our peace with God.

Romans 5:1 says, "Therefore, having been justified by faith, we have peace with God through our Lord Jesus Christ." Jesus died on the cross to make "shalom" or restitution for us with God.

Jesus is the Prince of Peace over God's kingdom of peace, of which the prophets foretold. The gospel of Jesus is "the gospel of peace" (Ephesians 6:15). Without Jesus, we would still be at enmity with God.

This peace with God delivers mental peace. "In peace I will both lie down and sleep, For You alone, O LORD, make me to dwell in safety" (Psalm 4:8). We can pillow our heads at night and sleep when we know that we have peace with God the Father through our Lord and Savior, Jesus Christ.

Do we treasure our peace? It has been said that we only truly value peace when we lose it. Remember David's mental anguish in Psalm 51 when he lost his peace with God? When we sin, we should read Psalm 51:1-2 again and pray this prayer, "Be gracious to me, O God, according to Your lovingkindness; According to the greatness of Your compassion blot out my transgressions. ²Wash me thoroughly from my iniquity And cleanse me from my sin." God will forgive us and make us at peace with Him. Then we accept that peace. Even say it, "I am at peace with God." Thank Him and praise Him.

Suggestions for further study: Do a word study of peace. Consider your life and make a list of things that shatter your peace and avoid them. "Seek peace and pursue it" (Psalm 12:14).

Daily Peace

Psalm 29:11 The LORD will give strength to His people; The LORD will bless His people with peace.
Psalm 85:8 I will hear what God the LORD will say; For He will speak peace to His people, to His godly ones; But let them not turn back to folly.

11

He Gives a Heart of Wisdom

So teach us to number our days,
That we may present to You a heart of wisdom.
Psalm 90:12

In Scripture, foolishness and wisdom are moral issues, not just intellectual ones. Wisdom motivates a righteous way of life and foolishness an evil one. According to Psalm 14:1, "The fool has said in his heart, 'There is no God.' They are corrupt, they have committed abominable deeds; There is no one who does good." However, the wise man knows God and lives a life of righteousness. Proverbs 9:10 says, "The fear of the LORD is the beginning of wisdom."

How can we live a life of wisdom that honors God instead of a foolish life that dishonors him? Let us look at one particular point. Moses says in Psalm 90:12, "So teach us to number our days, That we may present to You a heart of wisdom." Every day without God is a wasted day. Can we begin each day like David in Psalm 5:3, "In the morning, O LORD, You will hear my voice; In the morning I will order my prayer to You and eagerly watch"?

I Kings 3:10 says that it pleased the Lord when Solomon asked God for wisdom. God had told him to ask for whatever he wished, and he asked for an understanding heart to judge the people. How about us? Consider James 1:5: "But if any of you lacks wisdom, let him ask of God, who gives to all generously and without reproach, and it will be given to him." So, if it pleased the Lord for Solomon to ask for wisdom, won't it also please Him for us to ask for wisdom? Asking God for wisdom is an act of humility. It says, "I need your wisdom, O God."

"The testimony of the LORD is sure, making wise the simple" (Psalm 19:7b). When we sit down to study the Word of God, let us recognize it as the source of His wisdom, and thank Him that He gives it to us. Ask Him to grant us wisdom to apply the truth of His Word at the right time, in the right way, with the right attitude.

Proverbs 31:26 says of the virtuous woman, "She opens her mouth in wisdom, And the teaching of kindness is on her tongue." Oh, how often this is a struggle! It reminds us of Psalm 37:30: "The mouth of the righteous utters wisdom, And his tongue speaks justice." And do not forget to express wisdom when posting on social media.

Do you know godly men and women that stand out as wise? How would you describe them? James 3:13 describes the wise: "Who among you is wise and understanding? Let him show by his good behavior his deeds in the gentleness of wisdom." Then he continues in verse 17: "But the wisdom from above is first pure, then peaceable, gentle, reasonable, full of mercy and good fruits, unwavering, without hypocrisy." Now **that** is a heart of wisdom.

Suggestions for further study: Do we long for wisdom? It will not happen by accident; it is a lifelong endeavor. Study and pray for wisdom. Research question: were others in the Bible called wise?

Daily Wisdom

Psalm 19:7 The law of the LORD is perfect, restoring the soul; The testimony of the LORD is sure, making wise the simple.
Psalm 37:30 The mouth of the righteous utters wisdom, And his tongue speaks justice.
Psalm 49:3 My mouth will speak wisdom, And the meditation of my heart will be understanding.
Psalm 111:10 The fear of the LORD is the beginning of wisdom; A good understanding have all those who do His commandments; His praise endures forever.
Psalm 119:34 Give me understanding, that I may observe Your law And keep it with all my heart.
Psalms 119:104 From Your precepts I get understanding; Therefore I hate every false way.

12

He Takes Away All Fear

God is our refuge and strength, A very present help in trouble.
²Therefore we will not fear, though the earth should change
And though the mountains slip into the heart of the sea;
³Though its waters roar and foam,
Though the mountains quake at its swelling pride. *Selah.*
Psalms 46:1-3

Who could yearn for refuge and strength more than someone who is in constant danger? As we look at David's life, we know that was the case. For strength, David turned to God and often acknowledged Him as his refuge, his place of safety. What an example he leaves us of complete reliance on God.

All of us at times are at a loss. In the last year and a half, our world was turned upside down because of a pandemic. Consider other heartbreaks--a loved one is overtaken in sin and leaves the Lord. A child is ill. We may have financial difficulties. We could name a host of cares that cause us fear. It may also be that we have a dread that we cannot name. We just feel lost from the Lord, as if we have lost our moorings. God made us. He knows how subject to fear that we are, so He gave us a means to allay those fears.

David knew where to turn for refuge when troubles multiplied. In Psalms 46:1, David says, "God is our refuge and strength, a very present help in trouble." Some translations say "ever-present." It means He is always there. And then he describes the extent to which we can trust in God's protection in verses 2 and 3. "Therefore we will not fear, though the earth should change And though the mountains slip into the heart of the sea; ³Though its waters roar and foam, Though the mountains quake at its swelling pride." Can you picture the scene? Imagine standing on the mountains near the sea. The water begins to roar and foam, and the

31

mountains you are standing on start crashing down into the sea. David says he would not fear even if that were to happen. Why? Because he trusts in God.

Does trusting in God mean that nothing bad will ever happen to us? No, our figurative "mountains" might crash into the sea. We might lose our jobs, or get a terrible illness, or a thousand other things. But because we trust in God, we will overcome fear.

Does David literally mean that he would not be afraid, or does he mean that he will follow God despite the fear? Optimally, we will not fear. When fears arise, and they will, we will quell them through faith in the Lord. The phrase "fear not" is used at least 80 times in the Bible, most likely because God knows the enemy uses fear to diminish our resolve to serve Him. Fear can rob us of our joy **if we let it**. Remaining in fear is a choice. We can overcome fear through the power of the Lord and look to Him for comfort, peace, and wisdom, as we remember "be not dismayed whate'er betide, God will take care of you."

Suggestions for further study: Overcoming fear through faith in God is a common theme of the scriptures. Write Psalm 56:3-4 on a card and read it as a meditation over and over. Research question: find examples of people who were told not to fear.

Daily "No Fear"

Psalm 27:1-3 The LORD is my light and my salvation; Whom shall I fear? The LORD is the defense of my life; Whom shall I dread? [2]When evildoers came upon me to devour my flesh, My adversaries and my enemies, they stumbled and fell. [3]Though a host encamp against me, My heart will not fear; Though war arise against me, In spite of this I shall be confident.
Psalm 34:4 I sought the LORD, and He answered me, And delivered me from all my fears.
Psalm 56:3-4 When I am afraid, I will put my trust in You.[4]In God, whose word I praise, In God I have put my trust; I shall not be afraid. What can mere man do to me?

LESSON IV

Salvation Has Been Brought Down

NOTES

13

Restore My Soul

How blessed is he whose transgression is forgiven,
Whose sin is covered!
Psalm 32:1

Psalm 51 gives us tremendous insight into a heart broken by sin. When we read it, we experience David's raw grief and are reminded of our own pain and shame of sin. Yet there is also hope in this Psalm. David's urgent longing for God's grace and forgiveness is as poignant as his regret. It shows us a man fully aware of his burden of sin yet yearning for God's great compassion to blot it out. It is a great lesson for us, and we can pray along with David, "According to the greatness of Your compassion blot out my transgressions." And when we are tempted to sin, it is a good reminder of how heavy that burden will weigh on us. David's experience reminds us, "Don't do that. Remember how painful that was!"

Let us investigate this great Psalm.

Psalm 51:1-2 says, "Be gracious to me, O God, according to Your lovingkindness; According to the greatness of Your compassion blot out my transgressions. ²Wash me thoroughly from my iniquity And cleanse me from my sin."

David begins by calling for God's grace. (Some translations say mercy.) He knows that he does not deserve forgiveness. He recognizes God's lovingkindness and great compassion. He then asks God for cleansing—to blot out his transgressions. His sin has stained him, and he begs to be clean again.

Verses 3-4 say, "For I know my transgressions, And my sin is ever before me. ⁴Against You, You only, I have sinned And done what is evil in Your sight, So that You are justified when You speak And blameless when You judge."

David acknowledges his sin. This is not something he takes lightly. It is constantly on his mind. When he says, "against You, You only," David is not saying that he did not sin against Bathsheba or Uriah or others that he harmed with his sin, for he had. But it is his way of acknowledging the gravity of sinning against God. That should weigh heaviest on our hearts.. David also accepts responsibility for his sin when he says God is blameless. He is not blaming God for his transgressions.

Verses 7-13 say, "Purify me with hyssop, and I shall be clean; Wash me, and I shall be whiter than snow. [8] Make me to hear joy and gladness, Let the bones which You have broken rejoice. [9] Hide Your face from my sins And blot out all my iniquities. [10] Create in me a clean heart, O God, And renew a steadfast spirit within me. [11] Do not cast me away from Your presence And do not take Your Holy Spirit from me. [12] Restore to me the joy of Your salvation And sustain me with a willing spirit. [13] Then I will teach transgressors Your ways, And sinners will be converted to You."

David asks for restoration. "Purify me." "Wash me." "Restore to me the joy of Your salvation." There is no joy where he is—away from God—but he yearns for it. How beautiful these verses are. God does not want us to remain in the grief of sin. He wants to restore us to the joy of His salvation. We speak of someone being "restored" when they return in repentance to the Lord. Thank God for this restoration. What if we had no forgiveness for our sins? What a horrible situation. Rejoice for restoration back to God, just as the Ethiopian treasurer went on his way, rejoicing.

Suggestions for further study: The NASB calls this chapter "A Contrite Sinner's Prayer for Pardon." Make a list of other examples of "contrite sinners" we see in the scriptures.

Daily Contrition and Restoration

Read Psalms 51 often.

14

He Is Our Salvation

The LORD is my strength and song, And He has become my
salvation. [15]The sound of joyful shouting and salvation
is in the tents of the righteous.
Psalm 118:14-15a

Psalm 118 is a song of thanksgiving to God for His salvation. It
is taken from the Song of Moses, which was sung right after the
Exodus (Exodus 15:2). Imagine the joy of that time. The Israelites
had been on the brink of destruction before Pharaoh's army, and
the Lord performed the great miracle of parting the sea. "The
sound of joyful shouting and salvation is in the tents of the
righteous." Can you just picture their jubilation?

When God saved the Israelites from their physical enemies,
bringing them out of physical bondage, He intended it as a
representation of saving mankind from their sins through Christ,
bringing us out of spiritual bondage. Physical salvation of the
Israelites represents spiritual salvation through Christ. The Psalmist
may be speaking of deliverance from his enemies, but to us it
represents salvation from our bondage of sin. In 1 Corinthians 10:6,
11, Paul emphasized that these things were examples to us. The
writer to the Hebrews says that these are but the "shadow of good
things to come" (Hebrews 10:1).

After God parted the sea, the Israelites had to walk across to be
saved. "By faith they passed through the Red Sea as though they
were passing through dry land" (Hebrews 10:29). We ask the
question, "What do we have to do to be saved from our bondage of
sin?" In Acts 2, when the Jews realized that Jesus, whom they had
just crucified, was "both Lord and Christ," they were cut to the
heart and asked, "Brethren, what shall we do?" Peter answered,
"Repent, and each of you be baptized in the name of Jesus Christ

for the forgiveness of your sins; and you will receive the gift of the Holy Spirit" (Acts 2:36-38). Galatians 3:26-27 says, "For you are all sons of God through faith in Christ Jesus. [27]For all of you who were baptized into Christ have clothed yourselves with Christ."

We can relate to the Psalmist as he gives joyous thanks to God for His salvation. We praise God like the apostle Peter in 1 Peter 1:3-5, "Blessed be the God and Father of our Lord Jesus Christ, who according to His great mercy has caused us to be born again to a living hope through the resurrection of Jesus Christ from the dead, [4]to obtain an inheritance which is imperishable and undefiled and will not fade away, reserved in heaven for you, [5] who are protected by the power of God through faith for a salvation ready to be revealed in the last time."

Treasuring salvation strengthens our hearts. It keeps us focused on our Lord and His lovingkindness. Psalm 13:5-6 says, "But I have trusted in Your lovingkindness; My heart shall rejoice in Your salvation. [6]I will sing to the LORD, Because He has dealt bountifully with me." We need to thank God for our salvation.

Suggestions for further study: Research question: Is there an exhortation in the scriptures not to neglect or ignore our great salvation?

Daily Treasuring our Salvation

Psalm 9:14 That I may tell of all Your praises, That in the gates of the daughter of Zion I may rejoice in Your salvation.
Psalm 13:5 But I have trusted in Your lovingkindness; My heart shall rejoice in Your salvation.
Psalm 62:6-7 He only is my rock and my salvation, My stronghold; I shall not be shaken. On God my salvation and my glory rest; The rock of my strength, my refuge is in God.
Psalm 79:9 Help us, O God of our salvation, for the glory of Your name; And deliver us and forgive our sins for Your name's sake.
Psalm 96:2 Sing to the LORD, bless His name; Proclaim good tidings of His salvation from day to day.

15

A Savior Is Promised

For You will not abandon my soul to Sheol;
Nor will You allow Your Holy One to undergo decay.
Psalm 16:10 [Quoted in Acts 2:27]

Think of what it would have been like to be an Israelite in the time of David hearing of the prophecies of a coming Messiah. Would they sit in their "living rooms" and speculate about what they might mean, and when He might come? During their hard times of estrangement from God, what must it have been like to read these promises of a king to restore Israel? They may have wondered, "Will it be now? Will He come now?" We know that in Jesus' time, they had expectations of a Messiah. They had many false assumptions of what the Messiah would do when He came, but they expected Him.

In Matthew 22:42, Jesus posed a question to the Pharisees: "'What do you think about the Christ, whose son is He?' They said to Him, 'The son of David.'" It is clear they knew of the coming Messiah.

Similarly, John 7:31, 40-42 says, "But many of the crowd believed in Him; and they were saying, 'When the Christ comes, He will not perform more signs than those which this man has, will He?'... ⁴⁰Some of the people therefore, when they heard these words, were saying, 'This certainly is the Prophet.' ⁴¹Others were saying, 'This is the Christ.' Still others were saying, 'Surely the Christ is not going to come from Galilee, is He? ⁴²Has not the Scripture said that the Christ comes from the descendants of David, and from Bethlehem, the village where David was?'" So, they were looking for a Messiah to come. They knew some details of His coming, and some believed He might be Jesus.

Other examples of expectations of a Messiah coming include:

—Andrew said to his brother Simon Peter that they had found the Messiah (John 1:41).

—John sent his disciples to ask Jesus if he were the one to come (Matthew 11:3).

—Herod inquired of the chief priests and scribes after the visit from the wise men where Christ should be born (Matthew 2:4).

—John the Baptist said to those sent from Jerusalem, "I am not the Christ" (John 1:20), implying that there was to be a Christ.

—Even the Samaritan woman knew of the coming of the Messiah. "The woman said to Him, 'I know that Messiah is coming (He who is called Christ); when that One comes, He will declare all things to us'" (John 4:25).

How would they have known of this coming Messiah? They had read of it in the Old Scriptures, many times in the poetic language of the Psalms that they sang. In most of these prophecies, there are two levels of meaning-- the first is historical, related to the happenings of the time, and the second is prophetic, pointing to Jesus. Twenty-five different Psalms include at least one prophecy about the coming Messiah. Out of all the verses in the Old Testament, the most frequently quoted in the New Testament is the prophecy of Psalm 110:1, "The LORD says to my Lord: 'Sit at My right hand Until I make Your enemies a footstool for Your feet."

The Psalms has no greater purpose than to tell of the coming Messiah. We must realize that significance. Jesus said just prior to his ascension in Luke 24:44, "These are My words which I spoke to you while I was still with you, that all things which are written about Me in the Law of Moses and the Prophets, and the Psalms must be fulfilled." The fact that He fulfilled these prophecies is one of the keystone evidences that Jesus is the Christ.

Suggestions for further study: Study the Messianic prophecies found in Psalms and their fulfillment. Some important ones are listed on the next pages.

Daily Study of the Messianic Prophecies from Psalms

	Prophecy	Fulfillment
His Lineage		
From the Lineage of David	Psalm 89:3-4, 29-36; 132:11-17	Matthew 1:1-17; Luke 3:23-38
His Nature		
Son of God	Psalm 2:7	Luke 1:31-35; Matthew 3:16-17; Hebrews 1:5-6
Called King of the Jews	Psalm 2:6	John 12:12-13; 18:32
Is God	Psalm 45:6-7b	Hebrews 1:8-9
Will Call God His Father	Psalm 89:26	Matthew 11:27
Only "Begotten" Son of God	Psalm 89:27	Mark 16:6; Colossians 1:18; Revelation 1:5
Eternal	Psalm 102:25-27a	Revelation 1:8; Hebrews 1:10-12
Creator of All Things	Psalm 102:25-27b	John 1:3; Ephesians 3:9; Hebrews 1:10-12
Lord and King	Psalm 110:1a;	Matthew 22:41-45
Priest like unto Melchizedek	Psalm 110:4	Hebrews 6:17-20
Stone Rejected by the Builders	Psalm 118:22	Matthew 21:42-43
His Ministry:		
Infants Praise Him	Psalm 8:2	Matthew 21:15-16
Teach in Parables	Psalm 78:2	Matthew 13:34-35
His Death		
Conspire Against Him	Psalm 2:1-3	Matthew 26:3-4; Mark 3:6
Betrayed by Disciple	Psalm 41:9	Mark 14:17-18
Pray Before His Death	Psalm 22:2	Matthew 26:38-39

Despised and Rejected by His Own	Psalm 22:6-8	Luke 23:21-23
Hated w/o cause	Psalm 35:19	John 18:19-23; 15:24-25
Many Attempts to Kill Him	Psalm 31:13	Matthew 27:1
Accused by False Witnesses	Psalm 27:12; 35:11; 109:2	Matthew 26:59-61
Mocked	Psalm 22:7	Matthew 27:39
Unbelievers Scoff	Psalm 22:8	Matthew 27:41-43
Abandoned by His Disciples	Psalm 22:11	Mark 14:50
Blood and Water	Psalm 22:14a	John 19:34
Crucified	Psalm 22:14b	Matthew 27:35
Feel Forsaken by God	Psalm 22:1b	Mark 15:34
Thirst	Psalm 22:15	John 19:28
Hands and Feet Will Be Pierced	Psalm 22:16	John 20:25
Lots Cast for Garments	Psalm 22:18	John 19:23-24
"Into thy Hands"	Psalm 31:5	Luke 23:46
No Bones Broken	Psalm 34:20	John 19:32-33
Silent Before Accusers	Psalm 38:13–14	Matthew 26:62-63
Offered Gall/Vinegar	Psalm 69:21a	Matthew 27:34,48
Betrayer Replaced	Psalm 109:8b	Acts 1:20-26
His Resurrection and Ascension		
Resurrected	Psalm 16:8-10a	Acts 2:25-32
Body Not See Corruption	Psalm 16:8-10b	Acts 13:35-37
Ascension	Psalm 68:18a	Luke 24:51; Acts 1:9
Right Hand of God	Psalm 80:17; 110:1	Acts 5:31

16

Warnings Against Evil

Depart from evil and do good; Seek peace and pursue it.
Psalm 34:14

The Psalms have given us abundant encouragement and inspiration so far in this study. They also give us many warnings against doing evil, and we would be foolhardy if we neglected them. They are there to cause us to do right, not evil. If you were in physical danger, for instance, if your house were on fire, wouldn't you want someone to warn you? When you are warned, it would be foolish to ignore it. Thank you, Father, for these warnings in the Psalms.

The consequence of evil is separation from the Lord. Psalm 34:16 states, "The face of the LORD is against evildoers, To cut off the memory of them from the earth." Turning His face is figurative language, denoting either accepting or rejecting us. God will not even look at those who do evil. We do not want God's rejection; surely, we desire God's approval. 2 Timothy 2:15 tells us to be diligent to show ourselves approved unto God. We must always remember that the Lord created us to be near Him. He says if we will draw near to Him, He will draw near to us (James 4:8), but He will not let us near Him if we serve evil.

Psalm 7:14 describes the wicked man. "Behold, the wicked man conceives evil and is pregnant with mischief and gives birth to lies" (ESV). Consider that powerful image. Imagine someone pregnant with mischief; they conceive evil and give birth to lies or deceit. This sounds like someone desperate to figure out a way to cause trouble or harm others to benefit himself.

The next two verses say more about him, "He makes a pit, digging it out, and falls into the hole that he has made. His mischief returns upon his own head, and on his own skull his violence descends." All that evil scheming is like digging a pit and falling into it. Then all that evil falls right back on your head. I have known people like that. People who abuse alcohol and drugs often behave in this manner. They will do anything to get their fix. Eventually, they lose everything. They have dug an awful pit with the dirt falling back on their heads.

Do you want to ruin your life? Well, here is how. It is quite simple: devote your life to evil. Psalm 36:12 "There the doers of iniquity have fallen; They have been thrust down and cannot rise." I know some people that lie fallen, unable to rise. It describes some that I love dearly. It describes me without Christ. But we do not have to stay down. Christ raises us back up. He will get us out of that pit. 1 John 1:9: "If we confess our sins, He is faithful and righteous to forgive us our sins and to cleanse us from all unrighteousness." Praise the Lord, salvation has been brought down.

Suggestions for further study: Study Psalm 37.

Daily Warnings

Psalm 5:4 For You are not a God who takes pleasure in wickedness; No evil dwells with You.
Psalm 34:13 Keep your tongue from evil And your lips from speaking deceit.
Psalm 37:8 Cease from anger and forsake wrath; Do not fret; it leads only to evildoing.
Psalm 37:27 Depart from evil and do good, So you will abide forever.
Psalm 64:2 Hide me from the secret counsel of evildoers, From the tumult of those who do iniquity.
Psalm 119:101 I have restrained my feet from every evil way, That I may keep Your word.
Psalm 141:4a Do not incline my heart to any evil thing, To practice deeds of wickedness.

LESSON V

Blessed Be the Name

NOTES

17

Know That I Am God

Cease striving and know that I am God;
I will be exalted among the nations, I will be exalted in the earth.
Psalm 46:10

I am not sure we emphasize knowing God enough. We emphasize knowing His word, and we should. But we also need to know Him, as a Person. 2 Thessalonians 1:8 talks about how serious it is if we do not know God when Jesus returns, "dealing out retribution to those who do not know God and to those who do not obey the gospel of our Lord Jesus."

Think of the finest people that you know. How wonderful it is to know them. How would you describe them? I am sure you would describe their character, perhaps their humility, their great faith, and integrity. You might even say they are godly. Knowing them inspires us to be better people. What a loss you would experience if you had never known them. This is somewhat like our knowing God. We reflect on His characteristics that make Him the great God. How wonderful it is to know Him. "And those who know Your name will put their trust in You, For You, O LORD, have not forsaken those who seek You" (Psalm 9:10).

The Psalmists knew God. God revealed Himself through the Word so that we might also know Him. Knowing Jesus is knowing God. Hebrews 1:3 says Jesus is the "exact representation" of God the Father. When Jesus came, we saw the Father.

Jesus prayed that we would know God. In John 17:3, Jesus prayed, "This is eternal life, that they may know You, the only true God, and Jesus Christ whom You have sent. All through the Old Testament, God says that when people see the works that He performed, they "shall know that I am the LORD your God"

(Exodus 6:7; 16:12; 1 Kings 20:28; Ezekiel 20:20). Only the true God could work such works.

Knowing that there is a God and knowing God are two different things. Knowing God carries with it the idea of following Him and having a relationship with Him. I may know who a celebrity is, but I do not *know* that celebrity if I have no relationship with him or her.

We must be careful to know God as He is, and not as we want Him to be. For instance, if we do not believe that we must obey God to please Him, then we don't know Him. Titus 1:16 says that those who profess to know God but deny Him by their deeds are "detestable and disobedient and worthless for any good deed." Studying the Psalms will help us to know God as He is. It will help us to develop a loving, obedient relationship with Him.

Suggestions for further study: Read 1 John 4:6-8. It contains an essential element of knowing God.

Knowing God Daily

Psalm 25:4 Make me know Your ways, O LORD; Teach me Your paths.
Psalm 48:1-3 Great is the LORD, and greatly to be praised, In the city of our God, His holy mountain. ²Beautiful in elevation, the joy of the whole earth, Is Mount Zion in the far north, The city of the great King. ³God, in her palaces, Has made Himself known as a stronghold.
Psalm 67:1-2 God be gracious to us and bless us, And cause His face to shine upon us— *Selah*. ²That Your way may be known on the earth, Your salvation among all nations.
Psalm 77:14 You are the God who works wonders; You have made known Your strength among the peoples.
Psalm 100:3 Know that the LORD Himself is God; It is He who has made us, and not we ourselves; We are His people and the sheep of His pasture.
Psalm 135:5 For I know that the LORD is great And that our Lord is above all gods.

18

Understanding "Name"

O LORD, our Lord, How majestic is Your name in all the earth,
Who have displayed Your splendor above the heavens!
Psalm 8:1

In this section we cover some basic facts about the use of "name" in the scriptures and how name is used in reference to God. Then we will study about God's names. "Name" is a translation of the Hebrew word "shem" (in the Old Testament), and the Greek word "onoma" (in the New). Together, "name" appears around 1000 times and carries with it the idea of power, responsibility, purpose, and identity.

Frequently, in ancient times, a name expressed the essence and significance of what was being named. When Jesus said, "I have made Your name known to them, and will make it known" (John 17:26), He did not mean God's literal name, but that because they had known Jesus, they would know God's character and authority, His heart, mind, will, and being. Psalm 30:4 says, "Sing praise to the LORD, you His godly ones, And give thanks to His holy name." When we give thanks to His name, we are thanking Him. Another example is in Psalm 9:10: "And those who know Your name will put their trust in You, For You, O LORD, have not forsaken those who seek You." It is knowing His character that causes us to trust in Him.

Another interesting use of the word "name" is found in Matthew 28:19: "Go therefore and make disciples of all the nations, baptizing them in the name of the Father and the Son and the Holy Spirit." We are familiar with the expression, "Stop in the name of the law." The phrase means, "I represent the law. I tell you to stop by the authority of the law." In the same way, "baptizing them in the name" means, "I represent the Father, the Son and the Holy

Spirit." The baptism was accomplished by the apostles, and now by us, but when we baptize, we are representing the Father, the Son, and the Holy Spirit. Psalm 118:26 uses the expression in this way: "Blessed is the one who comes in the name of the LORD; We have blessed you from the house of the LORD."

We sometimes say that someone has a good name in the community. Proverbs 22:1 says, "A good name is to be more desired than great wealth, Favor is better than silver and gold." "Name" here means reputation, the esteem in which we are held. This is the use in Psalm 135:13: "Your name, O LORD, is everlasting, Your remembrance, O LORD, throughout all generations."

Another use of name is "for His name's sake." When God acts for his name's sake, it is for His reputation's sake. All our actions reflect on His name. It carries with it the same idea as, "Let your light so shine before men, that they may see your good works, and glorify your Father which is in heaven" (Matthew 5:16, KJV). When we glorify God, we are honoring His "name," or His reputation.

For His name's sake, God:
Guides us (Psalm 23:3; 31:3)
Delivers us from sin (Psalm 79:9)
Deals kindly with us (Psalm 109:21)
Revives us (Psalm 143:11)

Suggestions for further study: Do a word search for "name" in Psalms. Determine how it is being used.

Daily Study of Name

Psalm 5:11 But let all who take refuge in You be glad, Let them ever sing for joy; And may You shelter them, That those who love Your name may exult in You.
Psalm 20:5 We will sing for joy over your victory, And in the name of our God we will set up our banners. May the LORD fulfill all your petitions.
Psalm 31:3 For You are my rock and my fortress; For Your name's sake You will lead me and guide me.

19

Know His Name

And those who know Your name will put their trust in You, For
You, O LORD, have not forsaken those who seek You.
Psalms 9:10

God does not want to be something impersonal to us. He does
not want to be just a word in a book or some abstract thing out
there somewhere. Think of how God described David in Acts
13:22, "A man after my own heart, who will do all my will." I want
to have that kind of relationship with God, don't you? To do that,
we must meditate on Him more, reflect on our relationship more,
lean on Him more, and do His will because we trust Him more.

In the last section we studied how "name" can be used in
different ways. This section studies name as identification. In other
words, what should we call God? How should we identify Him?

Two words, God and LORD are the two most common names
given in scripture. In Genesis 1:1, "In the beginning, God created
the heavens and the earth," the word translated "God" is the word
"ĕlōhîm" (Strong's H430, a transliteration from Hebrew to Greek.)
The KJV translates this word in the following manner: God (2,346
times), god (244 times), judge (5 times), GOD (1 time), goddess (2
times), great (2 times), mighty (2 times), angels (1 time), exceeding
(1 time), God-ward (with H4136) (1 time), godly (1 time).

This is the more generic term for God. For instance, Genesis
3:5 (KJV): "For God [ĕlōhîm] doth know that in the day ye eat
thereof, then your eyes shall be opened, and ye shall be as gods,
[ĕlōhîm] knowing good and evil." Both God and gods are from this
same word. This word refers to both the true God and false gods.

In Genesis 2:4, the other main name for God, "YHWH," first appears. "YHWH" was transliterated into the Greek YĔHOVAH, and translated as LORD (in all capital letters) or Jehovah. "This is the account of the heavens and the earth when they were created, when the LORD [YĔHOVAH] God ['elohiym] made earth and heaven." The Hebrew word YHWH (Strong's H3068) is found 6,519 times and is usually translated as LORD or Jehovah, depending primarily on which version you are using. YHWH is by far the most often used name of God.

In Psalms "LORD" occurs in approximately 700 verses, "God" in approximately 350. As we read each verse below, let our hearts dwell on the characteristics of God that we read about. Let us praise God and give thanks for each one.

Suggestions for further study: Research question: How are we to treat God's name?

Knowing His Name Daily

Psalm 7:17 I will give thanks to the LORD according to His righteousness And will sing praise to the name of the LORD Most High.
Psalm 8:1 O LORD, our LORD, How majestic is Your name in all the earth, Who have displayed Your splendor above the heavens!
Psalm 20:7 Some boast in chariots and some in horses, But we will boast in the name of the LORD, our God.
Psalm 30:4 Sing praise to the LORD, you His godly ones, And give thanks to His holy name.
Psalm 34:3 O magnify the LORD with me, And let us exalt His name together.
Psalm 83:18 That they may know that You alone, whose name is the LORD, Are the Most High over all the earth.
Psalm 96:2 Sing to the LORD, bless His name; Proclaim good tidings of His salvation from day to day.
Psalm 135:3 Praise the LORD, for the LORD is good; Sing praises to His name, for it is lovely.
Psalm 139:20 For they speak against You wickedly, And Your enemies take Your name in vain.

20

The Great I AM

I, the LORD, am your God, Who brought you up from the land of
Egypt; Open your mouth wide and I will fill it.

Psalm 81:10

Perhaps the most important text in all the Bible for
understanding the meaning of the name YWHW (LORD or
Jehovah) is Exodus 3:13-15. God had just commanded Moses to go
to Egypt and to bring his people Israel out of captivity.

Verse 13 states, "Then Moses said to God, 'Behold, I am going
to the sons of Israel, and I will say to them, "The God of your
fathers has sent me to you." Now they may say to me, "What is His
name?" What shall I say to them?'"

Moses was going to a place where there were many gods, all
with different names. If he came and said, "God sent me to you,"
their immediate reaction may have been, "Which god?"

God answered this way in verse 14: "'I AM WHO I AM'; and
He said, 'Thus you shall say to the sons of Israel, "I AM has sent
me to you."'" In verse 15, He goes on to say that He is the LORD,
the God of their fathers, Abraham, Isaac, and Jacob. When God
said, "I AM WHO I AM" (the Hebrew verb, to be) He was
declaring His eternal and unchangeable self-existence, His unique
nature.

Let us consider another time that the name I AM was used in
the scriptures. In John 8:56–58, Jesus said to the Jews, "'Your father
Abraham rejoiced to see My day, and he saw it and was glad.' ⁵⁷So
the Jews said to Him, 'You are not yet fifty years old, and have You
seen Abraham?' ⁵⁸Jesus said to them, 'Truly, truly, I say to you,
before Abraham was born, I am.'"

Could Jesus have spoken any more exalted words? Could he have made any greater claim? The Great I AM had come to earth to dwell among men. He was claiming to be God, and the Jews did not miss it. They became so enraged that they picked up stones to stone him.

Do you remember what Thomas said when he put his hand into the side of the resurrected Christ in John 20:28? "My Lord and my God!" He recognized Jesus as Lord and God. Then Jesus made the great statement that applies to all of us. In verse 29, Jesus replied, "'Because you have seen Me, have you believed? Blessed are they who did not see, and yet believed.'" Yes, we believe that Jesus is Lord and God, the great I AM. Blessed be the name of the Lord.

Remember what Pharaoh said when Moses and Aaron told him that the Lord God said to let the people go? "'Who is the LORD, that I should obey His voice to let Israel go? I do not know the LORD, and besides, I will not let Israel go'" (Exodus 5:2). His statement implied that he understood that knowing the Lord would have required his obedience, as it does for us today.

Suggestions for further study: Make a list of hymns that relate to the name of God and find the lyrics. Example: *Jesus, Name Above all Names*

Knowing His Name Daily

In the KJV, the exact phrase "I am the LORD" occurs 162 times.

God spoke to Abraham: **Genesis 15:7** And he said unto him, I am the LORD that brought thee out of Ur of the Chaldees, to give thee this land to inherit it.
God spoke to Jacob: **Genesis 28:13** And, behold, the LORD stood above it, and said, I am the LORD God of Abraham thy father, and the God of Isaac: the land whereon thou liest, to thee will I give it, and to thy seed.
God spoke to Moses: **Exodus 6:2** And God spake unto Moses, and said unto him, I am the LORD.
Sixty-seven times in Ezekiel, God said that they will know that "I am the LORD."

LESSON VI

Hallelujah Praise Jehovah

NOTES

21

God, the Creator and Sustainer

The heavens are telling of the glory of God; And their expanse is declaring the work of His hands. [2]Day to day pours forth speech, And night to night reveals knowledge.

Psalm 19:1-2

Think of David in the fields, either tending his sheep or perhaps camping with his men before battle. He sees the heavens and marvels at God's handiwork, describing it with such rich imagery. Surely, we have all been observers of God's marvelous creation and felt the same. It is impossible for us who believe that God created the universe to believe it could have come about without a Designer.

Imagine taking a box of Legos and dumping them into the middle of the table. Look at the picture on the box and say, "Okay, we are going to watch the pieces just all come together by themselves to make this." That is more probable than the universe coming together without a designer and builder.

Why do so many deny that God created the universe or deny that He even exists? Perhaps it is because of what is said in Psalms 33:6-9: "By the word of the LORD the heavens were made, And by the breath of His mouth all their host. [7]He gathers the waters of the sea together as a heap; He lays up the deeps in storehouses. [8]Let all the earth fear the LORD; Let all the inhabitants of the world stand in awe of Him. [9]For He spoke, and it was done; He commanded, and it stood fast." Observe specifically, "Let all the earth fear the LORD; let all the inhabitants of the world stand in awe of him." If we believe that God is our creator, then we owe a responsibility to Him. We gain great blessings from acknowledging the Creator, but it also brings about responsibilities. Put them on a balance scale—what it costs versus what we gain. The costs pale in comparison to the gains. How could we live without the Lord?

Suggestions for further study: Psalm 8 is quoted four times in the New Testament—Matthew 21:16; Hebrews 2:5-8; 1 Corinthians 15:27; Ephesians 1:22. Read each and note the purpose of the teaching. Go outside and view the beauty and majesty of the earth and skies, and praise God the Creator. How great Thou art!

Daily Acknowledgment of Our Creator

Psalm 8:3-9 When I consider Your heavens, the work of Your fingers, The moon and the stars, which You have ordained; [4]What is man that You take thought of him, And the son of man that You care for him? [5]Yet You have made him a little lower than God And You crown him with glory and majesty! [6]You make him to rule over the works of Your hands; You have put all things under his feet, [7]All sheep and oxen, And also the beasts of the field, [8]The birds of the heavens and the fish of the sea, Whatever passes through the paths of the seas. [9]O LORD, our Lord, How majestic is Your name in all the earth!

Psalm 24:1-2 The earth is the LORD's, and all it contains, The world, and those who dwell in it. [2]For He has founded it upon the seas And established it upon the rivers.

Psalm 33:6 By the word of the LORD the heavens were made, And by the breath of His mouth all their host.

Psalm 74:16-17 Yours is the day, Yours also is the night; You have prepared the light and the sun. [17]You have established all the boundaries of the earth; You have made summer and winter.

Psalm 95:3-5 For the LORD is a great God And a great King above all gods, [4]In whose hand are the depths of the earth, The peaks of the mountains are His also. [5]The sea is His, for it was He who made it, And His hands formed the dry land.

Psalm 100:3 Know that the LORD Himself is God; It is He who has made us, and not we ourselves; We are His people and the sheep of His pasture.

Psalm 102:25 Of old You founded the earth, And the heavens are the work of Your hands.

Psalm 121:1-3 I will lift up my eyes to the mountains; From where shall my help come? [2]My help comes from the LORD, Who made heaven and earth. [3]He will not allow your foot to slip; He who keeps you will not slumber.

22

His Love Endures Forever

Surely goodness and lovingkindness will follow me all the days of
my life, And I will dwell in the house of the LORD forever.
Psalm 23:6

"For the LORD is good; His lovingkindness is everlasting And
His faithfulness to all generations" (Psalm 100:5). The idea here is
not just that God loves us, as glorious as that thought is, but He
loves us forever, no matter what! We can be assured that we can do
nothing to change that. Think of the father of the prodigal son. The
younger son was not just a young boy gone out to seek his fortune.
He had rejected his father. He demanded to be given what was
coming to him and left. Yet later in Luke 15:21-24, when the son
returned, there was no retaliation from the father for the rejection.
Instead, it was quite the opposite. His homecoming was a
celebration.

This is not to say that God will ignore our sins or that He loves
us too much to punish us. That kind of thinking is man's idea of
love. God's love gave His Son to save us even when we were
undeserving. Romans 5:8 (ESV) says, "But God shows his love for
us in that while we were still sinners, Christ died for us."

Even though God will not give up on us, we are not promised
another day. Today is the day of salvation. Remember Psalm 90:12:
"So teach us to number our days, That we may present to You a
heart of wisdom." Then we can live a blessed, joyous life with Him
in His kingdom.

God's unfailing love is a glorious thought. His mercy endures
forever! Every verse in Psalm 136 says, "For His lovingkindness is
everlasting." It is described as a "responsive" psalm. Responsive

psalms are the alternate singing of a text between the leader of a group and the rest of the group. Psalm 136:1-3 says:

Give thanks to the Lord, for He is good,
For His lovingkindness is everlasting.
²Give thanks to the God of gods,
For His lovingkindness is everlasting.
³ Give thanks to the Lord of lords,
For His lovingkindness is everlasting.

So how can we make our love toward God and toward others more "unfailing?" Does our mercy to others endure forever? That includes our spouse when he or she might annoy us, our children when they get on our last nerve (as we say in the South), friends, or strangers. We must have unfailing love for everyone. If we want to be more like God, we must practice unfailing love as He does.

Suggestions for further study: Read Psalm 136. Read it with your children or others as a responsive psalm.

Daily Unfailing Love

Psalm 103:17 But the lovingkindness of the LORD is from everlasting to everlasting on those who fear Him, And His righteousness to children's children.
Psalm 106:1 Praise the LORD! Oh give thanks to the LORD, for He is good; For His lovingkindness is everlasting.
Psalm 107:1 Oh give thanks to the LORD, for He is good, For His lovingkindness is everlasting.
Psalm 118:1-4 Give thanks to the LORD, for He is good; For His lovingkindness is everlasting. Oh let Israel say, "His lovingkindness is everlasting." Oh let the house of Aaron say, "His lovingkindness is everlasting." Oh let those who fear the Lord say, "His lovingkindness is everlasting."

23

The Lord Is Good to Us

I will sing to the LORD, Because He has dealt bountifully with me.
Psalm 13:6.

Even though the English word "providence" is not found in the scriptures, the concept certainly is. God's providence is defined as "the protective care of God." Notice that "provide" is contained in providence. God provides for us all. James 1:17 states, "Every good thing given and every perfect gift is from above, coming down from the Father of lights, with whom there is no variation or shifting shadow." God is so good to us.

God's providence is not a magic force field that keeps all good in and all bad out. Neither is God a genie granting all our wishes. Yes, God has the power to provide for us in this way, but we must remember that He loves us, wants the best for us, and knows what is better for us than we do. Think of the apostle Paul praying three times for a "thorn in the flesh" to be removed. God's answer is recorded in 2 Corinthians 12:9: "My grace is sufficient for you, for power is perfected in weakness." God may not take away the source of despair but will give peace and strength to overcome it. Can we pray, "Thy grace is sufficient"? We will be stronger if we do.

Remember when Isaac asked Abraham where the sacrifice was when on their way to offer Isaac? And do you remember Abraham's answer in Genesis 22:8? "Abraham said, 'God will provide for Himself the lamb for the burnt offering, my son.'" Then verse 14 says, "Abraham called the name of that place The LORD Will Provide, as it is said to this day, 'In the mount of the LORD it will be provided.'"

Oh, what great significance! The Lord provided a sacrifice in place of Isaac. And the Lord provides a sacrifice in place of us.

Remember the song *God is so Good* (by Paul Makai)?

God is so good, [sing three times], He's so good to me.
He saves my soul, [sing three times], and He makes me whole.
I praise His name, [sing three times], He's so good to me.

God's providence should prompt us to do likewise to others. On the sermon on the mount, Jesus said, "'You have heard that it was said, "You shall love your neighbor and hate your enemy." ⁴⁴But I say to you, love your enemies and pray for those who persecute you'" (Matthew 5:43-44). Then He says why in verses 45-46, "'So that you may be sons of your Father who is in heaven; for He causes His sun to rise on the evil and the good, and sends rain on the righteous and the unrighteous. ⁴⁶For if you love those who love you, what reward do you have?'" The lesson is that we should provide for others, even our enemies, because God provides for all.

We must be grateful for God's provisions. Read in Psalm 78:19-21 how God responded when the Israelites complained. We thank You, Father, for your provision for us.

Suggestions for further study: Write other verses to *God is so Good.* (Children especially enjoy this activity.) For example,
God made the world, [sing three times], He's so good to me.
God gives us food, [sing three times], He's so good to me.
Four syllables, [sing three times], He's so good to me.

Daily Recognition of God's Goodness to Us

Psalm 3:5 I lay down and slept; I awoke, for the LORD sustains me.
Psalm 68:10 Your creatures settled in it; You provided in Your goodness for the poor, O God.
Psalm 85:12 Indeed, the LORD will give what is good, And our land will yield its produce.
Palm 145:9 The LORD is good to all, And His mercies are over all His works.
Palm 145:15-16 The eyes of all look to you, and you give them their food in due season. ¹⁶You open your hand And satisfy the desire of every living thing.

24

God of Mercy

The Lord is gracious and merciful;
Slow to anger and great in lovingkindness.
Psalm 145:8

Mercy is a fundamental quality of God's nature, rooted in His love for us. He is merciful, in large part, because He is love. David calls God's mercy "great" in 2 Samuel 24:14, and Ephesians 2:4 says that God is rich in mercy. Mercy is the withholding of a just condemnation. As sinners, we deserve punishment (Romans 3:23). God's righteousness requires punishment for sin—He would not be holy otherwise. Since God loves us and is merciful, He sent His Son (John 3:16). Jesus received our just condemnation, and we received God's mercy. God's mercy is also rooted in His grace. Grace carries with it the idea of bestowing a gift or favor. Not to oversimplify, but mercy is withholding punishment that is deserved, whereas grace is bestowing a gift that is not deserved. "For all have sinned and fall short of the glory of God, [24]being justified as a gift by His grace through the redemption which is in Christ Jesus" (Romans 3:23-24).

Psalm 18:25a in the NKJV says, "With the merciful You will show Yourself merciful." NASB1995 uses "kind" rather than merciful. The lesson is, if we are merciful, God will be merciful to us, illustrated by the parable Jesus told in Matthew 18:23-35: "For this reason the kingdom of heaven may be compared to a king who wished to settle accounts with his slaves. [24]When he had begun to settle them, one who owed him ten thousand talents was brought to him. [25]But since he did not have the means to repay, his lord commanded him to be sold, along with his wife and children and all that he had, and repayment to be made. [26]So the slave fell to the ground and prostrated himself before him, saying, 'Have patience with me and I will repay you everything.' [27]And the lord of that slave felt compassion and released him and forgave him the debt. [28]But that slave went out and found one of his fellow slaves who owed him a hundred denarii; and he seized him and began to choke him, saying, 'Pay back what you owe.' [29]So his fellow slave fell to the ground and began to plead with him, saying, 'Have patience with me and I will repay you.' [30]But he was unwilling and went and threw him in prison until he should pay back what was owed. [31]So when his fellow slaves saw what had happened, they were deeply grieved and came and reported to their lord all that had happened. [32]Then summoning him, his lord said to him, 'You wicked slave, I forgave you all that debt because you pleaded with me. [33]Should you not also have had mercy on your fellow slave, in the same way that I had mercy on you?' [34]And his lord, moved with anger, handed him over to the torturers until he should repay all that was owed him. [35]My heavenly Father will also do the same to you, if each of you does not forgive his brother from your heart."

Where would we be without God's mercy? We would all be that first servant, heavy laden with massive debt that we cannot pay.

Suggestions for further study: To get mercy, we must give mercy. Mercy begins in a humble heart, with the thought, "There but for the grace of God go I." Find verses in the Bible that would help us develop mercy.

Daily Mercy (NKJV)

Psalm 6:2 Have mercy on me, O LORD, for I am weak; O LORD, heal me, for my bones are troubled.
Psalm 13:5 But I have trusted in Your mercy; My heart shall rejoice in Your salvation.
Psalm 85:7 Show us Your mercy, LORD, And grant us Your salvation.
Psalm 86:5 For You, Lord, are good, and ready to forgive, And abundant in mercy to all those who call upon You
Psalm 100:5 For the LORD is good; His mercy is everlasting, And His truth endures to all generations.

LESSON VII

How Great Thou Art

NOTES

25

Lord God Almighty

He who dwells in the of the Most High
Will abide in the shadow of the Almighty.
Psalm 91:1

One of our most beloved hymns, *Holy, Holy, Holy* (by Reginald Heber), begins, "Holy, holy, holy! Lord God Almighty."

"*El Shaddai*," Hebrew for God Almighty, appears 48 times in the scriptures. We often use the term "omnipotent" to describe this all-powerful aspect of God. The first time that we see it is in Genesis 17:1-2, "Now when Abram was ninety-nine years old, the LORD appeared to Abram and said to him, 'I am God Almighty; Walk before Me, and be blameless. [2]I will establish My covenant between Me and you, And I will multiply you exceedingly.'"

Psalm 115:3 says Almighty God does whatever he pleases without limits. "But our God is in the heavens; He does whatever He pleases." In Isaiah 46:9-10 God says, "'I am God and there is no one like me' . . . Saying, 'My purpose will be established, And I will accomplish all My good pleasure.'" Ultimately, the only thing that determines what God will accomplish and what He will not, is His own will. This is what it means to be almighty.

Remember the contest on Mt. Carmel? 1 Kings 18 is a great example of God's might. How ridiculous it is to even try to compete with God! No one and no thing can stop God from doing what He chooses to do. Daniel 4:35 says, "He does according to His will in the host of heaven and among the inhabitants of the earth; and no one can ward off His hand." (Read the context to see who said that. You might be surprised.) If God purposes to do a thing, it simply cannot be stopped by any power in the universe.

How reassuring this is. We do not serve a weak or insignificant God, but One who can do it all.

In fact, we cannot even imagine His powers. Ephesians 3:20-21 says, "Now to Him who is able to do far more abundantly beyond all that we ask or think, according to the power that works within us, [21]to Him be the glory in the church and in Christ Jesus to all generations forever and ever. Amen." His power is working within us. It is not that He is way out there somewhere. He is working within us to save us and sustain us.

How do we respond to God's infinite power? 1 Peter 5:6 says, "Therefore humble yourselves under the mighty hand of God, that He may exalt you at the proper time." We realize that without His almighty power, we can do nothing. "I am the vine, you are the branches; he who abides in Me and I in him, he bears much fruit, for apart from Me you can do nothing" (John 15:5).

Next time we sing, *Holy, Holy, Holy*, let us reflect on the meaning of Lord God Almighty.

Suggestions for further study: Do a word search for "power of God." Write down important points that you discover.

Daily Recognition of God's Power

Psalm 21:13 Be exalted, O LORD, in Your strength; We will sing and praise Your power.
Psalm 50:1 The Mighty One, God, the LORD, has spoken, And summoned the earth from the rising of the sun to its setting.
Psalm 63:2 Thus I have seen You in the sanctuary, To see Your power and Your glory.
Psalm 71:16 I will come with the mighty deeds of the Lord GOD; I will make mention of Your righteousness, Yours alone.
Psalm 89:6, 8a For who in the skies is comparable to the LORD? Who among the sons of the mighty is like the LORD... [8]O LORD God of hosts, who is like You, O mighty LORD?

26

The Most High God

I will give thanks to the LORD according to His righteousness
And will sing praise to the name of the LORD Most High.
Psalm 7:17

"Most High" occurs 50 times in the scriptures (NASB1995), over twenty in the Psalms. It recognizes the preeminence of God. He is highest: in rank, in title, and in position. He is highest in any of His attributes: in intelligence, goodness, mercy, etc. "Most High" conveys the idea of superiority, superior in every way to everything and everyone. Our response to this should be exaltation of Him. We recognize His position as the highest over all the heavens and the earth.

No pagan king ever recognized the "Most High" preeminence of the Lord more than King Nebuchadnezzar of Babylon. Recall the story in Daniel 3 of the golden statue. Nebuchadnezzar commanded all peoples to bow down and worship it or else be thrown into a furnace. After Shadrach, Meshach, and Abednego refused to bow down, King Nebuchadnezzar was furious, and asked them, "What god is there who can deliver you out of my hands?" Well, he was about to find out.

After the king saw them in the fire unharmed, he called them from the furnace, "Shadrach, Meshach and Abednego, come out, you servants of the Most High God, and come here!"

In Daniel 4:1-2, King Nebuchadnezzar wrote a letter relating his experiences. It begins, "Nebuchadnezzar the king to all the peoples, nations, and men of every language that live in all the earth: 'May your peace abound! ²It has seemed good to me to declare the signs and wonders which the Most High God has done for me.'" In the letter he told of a dream, Daniel's interpretation of it, and its fulfillment. He concluded the letter with these words in verse 37: "Now I, Nebuchadnezzar, praise, exalt and honor the King of heaven, for all His works are true and His ways just, and He is able to humble those who walk in pride."

Surely if a pagan King can recognize the preeminence of God, so can we!

Psalm 89:27 prophesies of Jesus, the Firstborn, coming to earth: "I also shall make him My firstborn, The highest of the kings of the earth." The Son of the Most High came to earth. The angel decreed to Mary of her Son in Luke 1:32: "He will be great and will be called the Son of the Most High; and the Lord God will give Him the throne of His father David."

"He is also head of the body, the church; and He is the beginning, the firstborn from the dead, so that He Himself will come to have first place in everything" (Colossians 1:18). Jesus has the preeminence of "first place in everything," When we give Jesus preeminence, we will devote our lives to him.

Suggestions for further study: Read Daniel 3-4. Contrast Nebuchadnezzar with the Pharaoh of Egypt.

Daily Recognition of God's Preeminence

Psalm 7:8 The LORD judges the peoples; Vindicate me, O LORD, according to my righteousness and my integrity that is in me.
Psalm 9:2 I will be glad and exult in You; I will sing praise to Your name, O Most High.
Psalm 57:2 I will cry to God Most High, To God who accomplishes all things for me.
Psalm 97:9 For You are the LORD Most High over all the earth; You are exalted far above all gods.

27

See His Splendor and Majesty

O LORD, our Lord,
How majestic is Your name in all the earth,
Who have displayed Your splendor above the heavens!
Psalm 8:1

There is such power and beauty in these words from Psalm 8. Majesty is a word reserved for the most royal. We address earthly kings as "Your Majesty." It was said of King Ahasuerus in Esther 1:4: "And he displayed the riches of his royal glory and the splendor of his great majesty for many days, 180 days." And Nebuchadnezzar said in Daniel 4:30: "Is this not Babylon the great, which I myself have built as a royal residence by the might of my power and for the glory of my majesty?"

We often talk about things of beauty being majestic, as in "experience the majesty of the Rockies." Similarly, splendor means magnificent in appearance and grandeur. These are terms the Psalmists used to describe God and His creation. We have read many accolades of Him, but these may be the pinnacle.

Consider Psalm 93:1: "The LORD reigns, He is clothed with majesty; The LORD has clothed and girded Himself with strength; Indeed, the world is firmly established, it will not be moved." The Lord is clothed, or arrayed, with majesty. Think of a king's clothing, how fine and ornate. The Lord's clothing is majesty. It is another figurative way to speak of the Lord's glory.

Psalm 45:3, 6-7 reads, "Gird Your sword on Your thigh, O Mighty One, In Your splendor and Your majesty...⁶Your throne, O God, is forever and ever; A scepter of uprightness is the scepter of Your kingdom.⁷You have loved righteousness and hated wickedness; Therefore God, Your God, has anointed You With the oil of joy above Your fellows." Do we know of whom this is speaking?

The Hebrew writer identifies this great king as Jesus when he says in Hebrews 1:8-9, "But of the Son He says…" and then quotes Psalm 45:6 that we read above. Read again the description of King Jesus. The king's scepter represents the authority of the king. "In Your splendor and Your majesty!" 1 Timothy 6:15 calls Him, "the blessed and only Sovereign, the King of kings and Lord of lords."

Majesty and splendor elevate the Lord to the highest of heights. We must not demean Him in anyway. He is not the "old man upstairs" or anything akin to it. Jesus is not our "bro." His name must not be used as a byword, empty of meaning or reverence. He is the king, clothed in majesty. We bow before the great I AM.

Suggestions for further study: David says in Psalm 145:5, "On the glorious splendor of Your majesty And on Your wonderful works, I will meditate." Let us meditate on this. Find songs that speak of the majesty or splendor of the Lord.

Daily Majesty and Splendor

Psalm 21:5 His glory is great through Your salvation, Splendor and majesty You place upon him.
Psalm 68:34 Ascribe strength to God; His majesty is over Israel And His strength is in the skies.
Psalm 90:16 Let Your work appear to Your servants And Your majesty to their children.
Psalm 96:6 Splendor and majesty are before Him, Strength and beauty are in His sanctuary.
Psalm 104:1 Bless the LORD, O my soul! O LORD my God, You are very great; You are clothed with splendor and majesty.
Psalm 145:11-13 They shall speak of the glory of Your kingdom And talk of Your power; [12] To make known to the sons of men Your mighty acts And the glory of the majesty of Your kingdom. [13] Your kingdom is an everlasting kingdom, And Your dominion *endures* throughout all generations.

28

Holy, Holy, Holy

Yet You are holy, O You who are enthroned
upon the praises of Israel.
Psalm 22:3

The holiness of God is one of the most prominent of all His divine characteristics. Holy means "sacred, Holy One, saint, set apart." It comes from a word meaning "to separate or cut off." God is separate from everything else. He is unique. He alone is God. In Isaiah 6:3, Isaiah had a vision where he saw angels: "And one called out to another and said, 'Holy, Holy, Holy, is the LORD of hosts, The whole earth is full of His glory.'"

The scriptures say that only God is holy. "For You alone are holy" (Revelation 15:4b). But aren't *we* told to be holy, also? How can we be holy if only God is holy? Think for a moment about the objects in scripture that are called holy. The Lord's temple is called holy. What made that building holy? In Exodus 28:2 and elsewhere, Aaron's garments were called holy garments. Again, what made the garments holy? In 1 Kings 8:4 and elsewhere, the tabernacle vessels were called holy. The seventh day was holy. Genesis 2:3: "Then God blessed the seventh day and sanctified it, because in it He rested from all His work which God had created and made." "Sanctified" is another word for separated or made holy.

What made all these objects holy? They were to be used only in God's service. They didn't gather in the temple for a school play or wear the holy garments to work on Monday. They didn't use the temple vessels to eat supper, and they didn't make Saturday just an ordinary day. God separated them all for His service, and this made them holy. God dictates what is holy. He said to man that these are to be made holy. They were to be used exclusively for His service.

In the same way that the objects are holy because God made them holy, we are holy because God has made us holy. We are separated or set apart for His service. As Peter wrote, we are a "holy nation" (1 Peter 2:9). The church, consisting of His people, belongs to God and is dedicated to His service. Peter also said, "But like the Holy One who called you, be holy yourselves also in all your behavior" (1 Peter 1:15). The holy objects could be defiled if they were used for secular purposes. In the same way, we defile ourselves if we do not live a life devoted to God and separated from sin. Just as in a marriage, where the couple is devoted solely to one another, we are devoted solely to God. That is our holiness. We sometimes think of holiness as purity, and purity will be a result of our holiness. But holiness describes our relationship with God.

God, being holy, is separate in His nature and character. God, in His holiness, will not be near sin. "But your iniquities have made a separation between you and your God, And your sins have hidden His face from you so that He does not hear" (Isaiah 59:2). Sin had separated us, but His Son brought us back, making us holy.

Let us reflect on the holiness of God. How Great Thou Art! There is none like Him. None can compare.

Suggestions for further study: Research question: How are we made holy or sanctified?

Daily Holiness

Psalm 11:4 The LORD is in His holy temple; the LORD's throne is in heaven; His eyes behold, His eyelids test the sons of men.
Psalm 15:1 O LORD, who may abide in Your tent? Who may dwell on Your holy hill?
Psalm 30:4 Sing praise to the LORD, you His godly ones, And give thanks to His holy name.
Psalm 99:3 Let them praise Your great and awesome name; holy is He.

LESSON VIII

To God Be the Glory

NOTES

29

Great Is Thy Faithfulness

Not to us, LORD, not to us but to your name be the glory,
because of your love and faithfulness.
Psalm 115:1 (NIV)

Before the Lord led His people into the Promised Land, He told them that He would deliver seven nations mightier than them unto them, and "you shall utterly destroy them" (Deuteronomy 7:2). He then gave them this reminder: "Know therefore that the LORD your God, He is God, the faithful God, who keeps His covenant and His lovingkindness to a thousandth generation with those who love Him and keep His commandments" (Deuteronomy 7:9). Even though they were not many in number or might, they took the land, just as God had said. He did what He said He would do.

In this context, faithful means that God is completely true to His word and true to His character. Compare Psalms 115:1 in the KJV below to the focus passage above from the NIV. "Not unto us, O LORD, not unto us, but unto thy name give glory, for thy mercy, and for thy truth's sake." Older translations will often translate faithful as true or truth. If God says that they will take the land, they will take the land. He is faithful and true to His word.

His faithfulness speaks to the core of His character. This means we can know for certain that He will do what He says He is going to do. He will do nothing out of His character, and we can know that the character we see Him display throughout Old and New Testament teachings remains today.

The following two New Testament passages show us how important the Lord's faithfulness is to us. "If we confess our sins, He is faithful and righteous to forgive us our sins and to cleanse us from all unrighteousness" (1 John 1:9). "Let us hold fast the confession of our hope without wavering, for He who promised is faithful" (Hebrews 10:23). The lesson for us is that even though people may let us down by lying to us or cheating us, God will never be unfaithful to who He is. This may be one of the characteristics of God that we undervalue. Imagine having a god that acts every day on His whims for that day. Our God is unchanging and faithful. You may be surprised how many times in the scriptures you will read of God's faithfulness.

We love the song, *Great is thy Faithfulness*. For those that live in Kentucky or Tennessee, it might be interesting that the songwriter Thomas Chisholm came from Franklin KY, a town right across the state line from our house. In the first verse it captures well the idea of God staying true to Himself:
Great is thy faithfulness, O God my Father;
There is no shadow of turning with thee;
Thou changest not, thy compassions, they fail not;
As thou hast been, thou forever wilt be.

Another meaning of the word faithful is steadfast. Psalm 31:23 reads, "O love the LORD, all you His godly ones! The LORD preserves the faithful And fully recompenses the proud doer."

Suggestions for further study: Do a word search for faithful. You will read of several admonitions to us to "be faithful." Where are we told to be faithful (steadfast) unto death?

Daily Faithfulness

Psalm 40:10-11 I have not hidden Your righteousness within my heart; I have spoken of Your faithfulness and Your salvation; I have not concealed Your lovingkindness and Your truth from the great congregation. [11] You, O LORD, will not withhold Your compassion from me; Your lovingkindness and Your truth will continually preserve me.
Psalm 43:3 O send out Your light and Your truth, let them lead me; Let them bring me to Your holy hill And to Your dwelling places.

30

The Lord Is Gracious

For the LORD is gracious and merciful;
Slow to anger and great in lovingkindness.
Psalm 145:8

Gracious is defined as showing favor or grace, which we frequently define as "unmerited favor." Sadly, we may have limited our appreciation of grace somewhat. Many times, we constrain God's grace to our salvation; we are saved by grace. And thanks be to God. But His grace also sustains us and blesses us in all that we do that is good and right. Our relationship with God and the Lord Jesus Christ is a great gift that He continually lavishes upon us by His grace. Listen to what the apostle Paul said in 1 Corinthians 15:10: "But by the grace of God I am what I am, and His grace toward me did not prove vain; but I labored even more than all of them, yet not I, but the grace of God with me." It was God's grace that made Paul the effective servant that he was.

"To this end also we pray for you always, that our God will count you worthy of your calling, and fulfill every desire for goodness and the work of faith with power, [12]so that the name of our Lord Jesus will be glorified in you, and you in Him, according to the grace of our God and the Lord Jesus Christ" (2 Thessalonians 1:11-12). By God's grace we live every day in a way that glorifies the name of Jesus. It is favor, a gift from God.

The Lord's grace was part of the beloved blessing that God gave to Moses for Aaron in Numbers 6:24-26. "The LORD bless you, and keep you; [25]The LORD make His face shine on you, And be gracious to you; [26]The LORD lift up His countenance on you, And give you peace."

Remember the story of Jonah? After Nineveh repented, it displeased Jonah that God decided not to destroy them. Jonah complained to God in Jonah 4:2, praying, "Please LORD, was not this what I said while I was still in my own country? Therefore, in order to forestall this I fled to Tarshish, for I knew that You are a gracious and compassionate God, slow to anger and abundant in lovingkindness, and one who relents concerning calamity." Is he saying, "I knew you wouldn't go through with it"? Instead of thanking God for his grace, he is complaining that God's grace prevented Him from bringing destruction on Jonah's enemies, and that angered him. When others receive great gifts from God, let us be thankful for God's grace towards all.

So when the Psalmists call the Lord gracious, they are recognizing this aspect of His character: He is gracious and giving in all good things. Notice that many times, they request grace of the Lord. "Be gracious, oh LORD…" (Psalm 6:2; 9:13; 27:7; 30:10; 31:9; 41:4, 10; 59:5; 86:3; 123:2-3).

Suggestions for further study: Read all of Paul's salutations to the churches and study his treatment of God's grace. Remember, these are not just idle icebreaker comments, but true, heart-felt greetings.

Daily Grace

Psalm 4:1 Answer me when I call, O God of my righteousness! You have relieved me in my distress; Be gracious to me and hear my prayer.
Psalm 25:16 Turn to me and be gracious to me, For I am lonely and afflicted.
Psalm 27:7 Hear, O LORD, when I cry with my voice, And be gracious to me and answer me.
Psalm 30:10 Hear, O LORD, and be gracious to me; O LORD, be my helper."
Psalm 84:11 For the LORD God is a sun and shield; The LORD gives grace and glory; No good thing does He withhold from those who walk uprightly.
Psalm 86:15 But You, O Lord, are a God merciful and gracious, Slow to anger and abundant in lovingkindness and truth.

31

God Is Good

Good and upright is the LORD;
Therefore He instructs sinners in the way.
Psalm 25:8

When we were very young children, we prayed the prayer: "God is great. God is good. And we thank Him for our food. By His hand we must be fed. Give us Lord our daily bread. Amen." God is good. What a simple, yet deeply profound statement. It is different from the statement that God is good to me. When we say God is good, we are talking about His character. He is good. Nothing that God does has to be justified as right or wrong because He defines good. We cannot say, God is too good to do that. If God does it, it is good. If you want to know whether something is good, compare it to God, who is the standard of good. Everything we call "good" is only truly good if it lines up with who God is or what He does.

Sometimes we hear it said, "God is good," as gratitude for answered prayers. It is good to recognize that "every good thing given and every perfect gift is from above, coming down from the Father of lights" (James 1:17). Let us also remember that God's goodness is not dependent on whether He gives us what we ask. God's goodness is an absolute. Yes, God is good, always and in all ways. "Oh give thanks to the LORD, for He is good, For His lovingkindness is everlasting" (Psalm 107:1).

Jesus recognized the goodness of God. "As He was setting out on a journey, a man ran up to Him and knelt before Him, and asked Him, 'Good Teacher, what shall I do to inherit eternal life?' [18]And Jesus said to him, 'Why do you call Me good? No one is good except God alone.'" (Mark 10:17-18). Now Jesus is not saying, "I am not good." Neither is He saying, "I am not God." Perhaps He was saying, "Are you acknowledging that I am God since you call me good, and God alone is good?"

None of us are good like God is. He made us good, but we choose to sin and do evil. We are to strive for goodness. God's goodness reminds us that God hates sin, not merely because it is a challenge to His authority, but because He seeks good for us. God knows that sin wrecks our lives. It separates us from Him, so He hates it. It brings other horrible consequences. "Good and upright is the LORD; Therefore, He instructs sinners in the way" (Psalm 25:8).

So once again, it is an extremely simple, but deeply profound thought: God is good. Let us praise His name, for He is good. Let us do good and not evil.

Suggestions for further study: Research questions: where do we find in the Bible that good overcomes evil? Where do we find that it is sin if we know to do good and do not do it?

Daily Recognition of God's Goodness

Psalm 16:2 I said to the LORD, "You are my Lord; I have no good besides You.
Psalm 34:8 O taste and see that the LORD is good; How blessed is the man who takes refuge in Him!
Psalm 34:10 The young lions do lack and suffer hunger; But they who seek the Lord shall not be in want of any good thing.
Psalm 52:9 I will give You thanks forever, because You have done it,
And I will wait on Your name, for it is good, in the presence of Your godly ones.
Psalm 54:6 Willingly I will sacrifice to You; I will give thanks to Your name, O LORD, for it is good.
Psalm 86:5 For You, Lord, are good, and ready to forgive, And abundant in lovingkindness to all who call upon You.
Psalm 100:5 For the LORD is good; His lovingkindness is everlasting And His faithfulness to all generations.
Psalm: 106:1 Praise the LORD! Oh give thanks to the LORD, for He is good; For His lovingkindness is everlasting.

32

Our Glorious God

I will give thanks to You, O Lord my God, with all my heart,
And will glorify Your name forever.
Psalm 86:12

We sing so often of the glory of God, and yet, it is not often that we try to understand what it is that we are singing about. The English word "glory" occurs 402 times in the KJV, so let us see what we can learn about this important quality of God. Even then, we will just touch the hem of the garment of the topic.

The English word glory means magnificence or great beauty. The glory of God is like a diamond with many dazzling facets. Imagine holding a diamond up to the light and seeing its beauty. That is a tiny taste of witnessing the glory, the beauty, the light of God.

"The heavens are telling of the glory of God; And their expanse is declaring the work of His hands. 2Day to day pours forth speech, And night to night reveals knowledge" (Psalm 19:1-2). What are the heavens saying? They are telling us of the glory of God. We see it every day—the glory of His creation. To God be the glory. Great things He hath done. Just look around at creation. It is glorious, just beautiful. Open your eyes. The Lord is like this, only better.

John 1:14 says, "And the Word became flesh, and dwelt among us, and we saw His glory, glory as of the only begotten from the Father, full of grace and truth."

2 Corinthians 4:6 (NIV) says, "For God, who said, 'Let light shine out of darkness,' made his light shine in our hearts to give us the light of the knowledge of God's glory displayed in the face of Christ." Let us read that several times. Picture it. God made light

shine into our hearts, and we can see God's glory by looking into the face of Jesus, not literally, of course, but spiritually. When we see Jesus, we see the Father in all His glory. So, to see His glory, we look at creation and we look into the "face" of Jesus. It is as if the Father is saying, "I am glorious. Just open your eyes and see."

Many times, God's glory is described as something to be seen. The passage above in John says, "We saw His glory." The passage above in 2 Corinthians says it is "displayed" in the face of Jesus. Open your eyes and see the beauty of the Lord. "Seeing" it is recognizing it, appreciating it, and valuing it. Our God is glorious in His holiness, in His uniqueness, and in everything that He is. Look at all these characteristics that we are studying about God. Just look and see! He is glorious!

We have a responsibility to give glory to God. It is said of Abraham, "Yet, with respect to the promise of God, he did not waver in unbelief but grew strong in faith, giving glory to God" (Romans 4:20). Psalms 86:12 says, "I will give thanks to You, O Lord my God, with all my heart, And will glorify Your name forever." We must not tarnish the beauty and glory of God.

Suggestions for further study: Study more about our responsibility to glorify God. Read Matthew 5:16 and 2 Corinthians 3:18.

Daily Glory of God

Psalm 24:10 Who is this King of glory? The LORD of hosts, He is the King of glory. *Selah.*
Psalm 29:2 Ascribe to the LORD the glory due to His name; Worship the LORD in holy array.
Psalm 66:2 Sing the glory of His name; Make His praise glorious.
Psalm 72:19 And blessed be His glorious name forever; And may the whole earth be filled with His glory. Amen, and Amen.
Psalm 87:3 Glorious things are spoken of you, O city of God. *Selah.*
Psalm 105:3 Glory in His holy name; Let the heart of those who seek the LORD be glad.

LESSON IX

The Battle Belongs to the Lord

NOTES

33

The LORD Hears

In the morning, O LORD, You will hear my voice;
In the morning I will order my prayer to You and eagerly watch.
Psalm 5:3

The Hebrew word for hear is "shema," but it actually means to hear and act upon what was heard. When the scriptures say that God hears us, it means that He is acting upon what He hears. In prayer, we call upon the mightiest, most loving and merciful being in the universe, and He hears and acts upon our prayers.

Paul said in Romans 10:1, "My heart's desire and my prayer to God..." The most basic definition of prayer is "talking to God." Prayer is not just meditation on spiritual thoughts or even on the Word; it is directly speaking to God. It is the communication of the human soul with the Lord who created that soul.

So many times David begged God to hear his prayers. David wasn't expressing doubt that God would hear him, but rather it was David's way of recognizing his great need of God and acknowledging the great blessing that the Sovereign God would hear him.

We must realize the magnificence and love of the One with whom we are speaking. Would we go to a great general and tell him how he should fight a war? Would we go to the world's best chef and show him how to make an omelet? We should trust God more and learn the true meaning of "Thy will be done." Prayer is not a frantic pleading with God to do what we want. We pour out our heart's desire, but then when we say, "Thy will be done," it means we trust Him to understand and do what is best for us.

So as we pray today, let us set our heart on seeking God's will rather than God doing ours. Let us praise and give thanks. Let us know that He loves us more than we can possibly appreciate and that He wants good for us in all things. If we truly believe that, we will put our trust in Him when we pray.

The song *Dear Lord and Father of Mankind* (by John G. Whittier) is a prayer that can reach from our hearts to God's:

Dear Lord and Father of mankind,
Forgive our foolish ways;
Reclothe us in our rightful mind,
In purer lives thy service find,
In deeper reverence, praise.

Suggestions for further study: Make a list of songs that are prayers or written in the first person. For instance, *I Surrender All,* (by Judson W. Van DeVenter). A verse and refrain are below:

All to Jesus I surrender, All to him I freely give;
I will ever love and trust him, In his presence daily live.
Refrain: I surrender all, I surrender all,
All to thee, my blessed Savior, I surrender all.

God Hears Daily

Psalm 10:17 O LORD, You have heard the desire of the humble; You will strengthen their heart, You will incline Your ear
Psalm 17:1 Hear a just cause, O LORD, give heed to my cry; Give ear to my prayer, which is not from deceitful lips.
Psalm 27:7 Hear, O LORD, when I cry with my voice, And be gracious to me and answer me.
Psalm 34:17 The righteous cry, and the LORD hears And delivers them out of all their troubles.
Psalm 55:19 God will hear and answer them—Even the one who sits enthroned from of old—*Selah*. With whom there is no change, And who do not fear God.
Psalm 66:19 But certainly God has heard; He has given heed to the voice of my prayer.
Psalm 77:1 My voice rises to God, and I will cry aloud; My voice rises to God, and He will hear me.

34

God Our Help

I will lift up my eyes to the mountains; From where shall my help
come? [2]My help comes from the LORD,
Who made heaven and earth.
Psalm 121:1-2

Observe how many entreaties for God's help are found as you
read the Psalms. For instance, read Psalm 28:2: "Hear the voice of
my supplications when I cry to You for help, When I lift up my
hands toward Your holy sanctuary." The word "cry" here implies a
call out for help. Imagine standing in a burning building calling for
help. This is a plea to God to help us with something that we
cannot do on our own.

Is God our Helper today or just in olden times? In 2
Corinthians 6:2, Paul quotes from Isaiah 49:8. It says, "For He says,
'At the acceptable time I listened to you, And on the day of
salvation I helped you...'" When is the day of salvation that Isaiah
spoke of? Paul tells us. "Behold, now is 'the acceptable time,'
behold, now is 'the day of salvation.'" We cannot save ourselves.
Romans 5:6 says, "For while we were still helpless, at the right time
Christ died for the ungodly." We were helpless to save ourselves. So
God sent His Son. He is our Help.

Does He help us to avoid temptation? Does He help when we
are distraught? Why would we pray if He did not help us? Let us
use the examples from Psalms to ask God for help:

1) Acknowledge to God that we need Him and want His help.
Psalm 5:2: "Heed the sound of my cry for help, my King and my
God."

2) Admit humbly that we need Him. Psalm 40:17: "Since I am afflicted and needy, Let the Lord be mindful of me. You are my help and my deliverer; Do not delay, O my God."

3) Ask the Lord for protection. Psalm 16:1-2: "Preserve me, O God, for I take refuge in You. ²I said to the LORD, 'You are my Lord; I have no good besides You.'"

4) Thank Him for His help. Psalm 28:7: "The LORD is my strength and my shield; My heart trusts in Him, and I am helped; Therefore, my heart exults, And with my song I shall thank Him."

Asking for the Lord's help is recognition of our reliance on Him. Why would we even try to make it without Him?

Suggestions for further study: What do we need help with? To answer that question, we must search our hearts. What are our heart problems? Do we ignore God too much? Do we have problems with selfishness? Are we satisfied with our spiritual growth? Ask for help, then praise and thank God.

Daily Help

Psalm 22:19 But You, O LORD, be not far off; O You my help, hasten to my assistance.

Psalm 30:2 O LORD my God, I cried to You for help, and You healed me.

Psalm 42:5 Why are you in despair, O my soul? And why have you become disturbed within me? Hope in God, for I shall again praise Him For the help of His presence.

Psalm 46:1 God is our refuge and strength, A very present help in trouble.

Psalm 71:12 O God, do not be far from me; O my God, hasten to my help!

Psalm 102:1 Hear my prayer, O LORD! And let my cry for help come to You.

Psalm 118:7 The LORD is for me among those who help me; Therefore I will look with satisfaction on those who hate me.

Psalm 119:147 I rise before dawn and cry for help; I wait for Your words.

35

Shield About Me

But You, O LORD, are a shield about me,
My glory, and the One who lifts my head.
Psalm 3:3

A hymn of great praise is *A Shield about Me* (by Donn Thomas and Charles Williams). It is Psalm 3:3 set to music. Tears come as the chorus swells, "Hallelujah. Hallelujah," and joyous praise wells up in the heart. Psalm 3 was written by David. Most scholars seem to believe that it describes his fleeing for his life from his son Absalom. One writer has called this time period "the darkest days of David's life." Imagine not only having to flee for your life, but from your own son.

David begins this Psalm in prayer to God (verses 1-2): "O LORD, how my adversaries have increased! Many are rising up against me. ²Many are saying of my soul, 'There is no deliverance for him in God.' *Selah.*" Just think of it: people were saying, "There is no deliverance for him in God." What could be worse?

We read more about this in 2 Samuel 15:13, where David was told, "The hearts of the men of Israel are with Absalom," meaning against David. Regardless of what they said, David did not lose hope in God's ability or willingness to deliver him. Back to Psalm 3 (verses 3-4): "But You, O LORD, are a shield about me, My glory, and the One who lifts my head. ⁴I was crying to the LORD with my voice, And He answered me from His holy mountain. *Selah.*"

It does not sound like David believed his enemies—that there is no deliverance in the Lord, does it? He spoke to the Lord, "You, O Lord are a shield about me." This was a man frequently in battle. Just imagine how powerful it was for the great soldier to call God his shield. Shield implies protection in battle, and David implies total protection when he says the Lord is a shield about him. He is surrounded by the protection of the Lord. He goes on to say that God is his glory, even in a time when his earthly glory has been taken from him. God is the lifter of David's head. The head, in time of trouble and sorrow, is naturally bowed down, as if overpowered with the weight of affliction. See Psalm 35:14: "I bowed down mourning, as one who sorrows for a mother." Psalm 38:6: "I am bent over and greatly bowed down; I go mourning all day long." To lift the head, therefore, means to relieve burdens and sorrow.

In Psalm 3:4, David turned to the Lord: "I was crying to the LORD." And the Lord answered his cries. The Lord was faithful to David, just as He is faithful to us. Do you think that David really believed this? Did he really have that much trust in God or were these flowery words?

What about us? Do we believe David's words? Do we face enemies today? 1 Peter 5:8 says, "Be of sober spirit, be on the alert. Your adversary, the devil, prowls around like a roaring lion, seeking someone to devour." Do we see the Lord as a shield about us? Ephesians 6 describes the "full armor of God." Do you remember what the shield was? Verse 6 tells us. "In addition to all, taking up the shield of faith with which you will be able to extinguish all the flaming arrows of the evil one." Truly David had the shield of faith, and so must we.

Suggestions for further study: "Shield" is found about 20 times in Psalms. Do a search to find them all.

Daily Shield

Psalm 5:12 For it is You who blesses the righteous man, O LORD, You surround him with favor as with a shield.
Psalm 7:10 My shield is with God, Who saves the upright in heart.
Psalm 18:2 The LORD is my rock and my fortress and my deliverer, My God, my rock, in whom I take refuge; My shield and the horn of my salvation, my stronghold.

36

A Mighty Fortress

I love You, O LORD, my strength, The LORD is my rock and my fortress and my deliverer, [2]My God, my rock, in whom I take refuge; My shield and the horn of my salvation, my stronghold.
Psalm 18:1-2

The introduction to Psalm 18 (NASB1995) says, "The LORD Praised for Giving Deliverance. For the choir director. A Psalm of David the servant of the LORD, who spoke to the LORD the words of this song in the day that the LORD delivered him from the hand of all his enemies and from the hand of Saul."

David recognized the source of the victory when he says, "The LORD is my rock and my fortress and my deliverer." Psalms like this remind us of David's epithet, "a man after God's own heart." Many kings after a battle stand before the people to proudly receive laud and praise for victory, but not David. He humbly credits the Lord.

Even as a young man, when David prepared to go to fight Goliath in 1 Samuel 17:37, he said, "The LORD who delivered me from the paw of the lion and from the paw of the bear, He will deliver me from the hand of this Philistine." Then to Goliath as he stood before him, he declared, "And that all this assembly may know that the LORD does not deliver by sword or by spear; for the battle is the LORD's, and He will give you into our hands" (1 Samuel 17:47).

Remember when Gideon went to battle with the Midianites in Judges 7, and God narrowed the army from 32,000 to 300? The Lord told Gideon: "The people who are with you are too many for Me to give Midian into their hands, for Israel would become boastful, saying, 'My own power has delivered me'" (Judges 7:2). The battle belongs to the Lord.

The Psalms were written in days when fortresses were critical to military defense strategy. They would find for themselves a safe, strong place to hide from the enemy, especially when they were under attack. David says that for him, God was that place. God was his fortress.

How is God our fortress today? Paul gives the answer in Ephesians 6:10-11: "Be strong in the Lord and in the strength of His might. ¹¹Put on the full armor of God, so that you will be able to stand firm against the schemes of the devil." Satan is our Goliath. We are in constant battle with him. Remember that David said to Goliath: "The LORD does not deliver by sword or by spear; for the battle is the LORD's." (1 Samuel 17:47).

Think of the hymn *A Mighty Fortress is Our God* (by Martin Luther) and see the great battle captured in it.

A mighty fortress is our God, a bulwark never failing;
Our Helper He, amid the flood of mortal ills prevailing.
For still our ancient foe does seek to work us woe;
His craft and power are great, and, armed with cruel hate,
On earth is not his equal.

Suggestions for further study: Search your heart and find your Goliath. Is your Goliath bitterness, a sharp tongue, pride, jealousy, or worry? Is it anger or an unforgiving heart? Read the Bible and pray. The battle belongs to the Lord.

Daily Fortress

Psalm 31:3 For You are my rock and my fortress; For Your name's sake You will lead me and guide me.
Psalm 71:3 Be to me a rock of habitation to which I may continually come; You have given commandment to save me, For You are my rock and my fortress.
Psalm 91:2 I will say to the LORD, "My refuge and my fortress, My God, in whom I trust!"

Lesson X

There Is a God

NOTES

37

Our God Is an Awesome God

For the LORD Most High is awesome, the great
King over all the earth.
Psalm 47:2 (NIV)

What is meant when the scriptures say our God is an awesome God? In our times, we use "awesome" as a synonym for wonderful. We might say, "He is an awesome teacher," and we mean the best! Is that what the scriptures mean when they call God an awesome God?

It is interesting that "awesome" does not appear in the KJV of the scriptures. For instance, instead of awesome in Psalm 47:2, the KJV says, "For the LORD most high is terrible; he is a great King over all the earth" (Compare to the focus verse above in the NIV). To us, terrible means extremely or distressingly bad, the absolute opposite of awesome. We might say, "He is a terrible teacher," meaning the worst! So how can one word translate as opposites in different translations?

In Deuteronomy 7, Moses reassures the Israelites that they did not have to be afraid of their enemies because God would protect them with His mighty powers. He says in Deuteronomy 7:21, "Thou shalt not be affrighted at them: for the LORD thy God is among you, a mighty God and terrible" (KJV). The NIV translates this as, "Do not be terrified by them, for the Lord your God, who is among you, is a great and awesome God." A "terrible" God causes terror in the hearts of those who would oppose Him. An "awesome" God causes awe for the same reason. It is the same concept.

God is also awesome in the sense of wonderful, tremendous, and too marvelous for words. And we study that aspect of Him in other lessons. But when we read the word awesome in the scriptures, it is speaking specifically of the awe and terror that His great and powerful acts should generate in all mankind.

Are we to fear this terrible/awesome God? If we are not living our lives devoted to God, then yes, we should fear the consequences of that. Matthew 10:28 warns, "Do not fear those who kill the body but are unable to kill the soul; but rather fear Him who is able to destroy both soul and body in hell." We know that is not what God wants. Romans 6:23 says, "For the wages of sin is death, but the free gift of God is eternal life in Christ Jesus our Lord."

Suggestions for further study: Does God want us to live in fear of Him? Find scriptures that back up your beliefs.

God Is Awesome Daily

Psalm 65:5 By awesome deeds You answer us in righteousness, O God of our salvation, You who are the trust of all the ends of the earth and of the farthest sea.
Psalm 66:3 Say to God, "How awesome are Your works! Because of the greatness of Your power Your enemies will give feigned obedience to You.
Psalm 89:6-8 For who in the skies is comparable to the LORD? Who among the sons of the mighty is like the LORD, [7]A God greatly feared in the council of the holy ones, And awesome above all those who are around Him? [8]O LORD God of hosts, who is like You, O mighty LORD? Your faithfulness also surrounds You.
Psalm 99:3 Let them praise Your great and awesome name; Holy is He.
Psalm 106:21-22 They forgot God their Savior, Who had done great things in Egypt, [22]Wonders in the land of Ham And awesome things by the Red Sea.
Psalm 111:9 He has sent redemption to His people; He has ordained His covenant forever; Holy and awesome is His name.
Psalm 145:6 Men shall speak of the power of Your awesome acts, And I will tell of Your greatness.

38

The Lord Is Righteous and Just

For the LORD is righteous, He loves righteousness;
The upright will behold His face.
Psalm 11:7

The works of His hands are truth and justice;
All His precepts are sure.
Psalm 111:7

What does it mean to say that the Lord is righteous or just?
What is the impact of these characteristics on us?

The righteousness of God is virtually synonymous with His justice. When we say that God is righteous and just, we are saying that He always does what is right, what should be done, and that He does it consistently, without partiality or prejudice. The word just and the word righteous are synonymous in both the Old and New Testaments. Sometimes the translators render the same original word "just" and other times "righteous" with no distinction that we can ascertain. Because God defines justice and righteousness, it is impossible for Him to be unjust or unrighteous. If God does it, it is right. It is fair.

We stand before a righteous and just judge. We never have to question whether God's judgement is fair or if He is being righteous in his treatment of us. His mercy does not preclude His justice. God does not set aside His justice to grant mercy. There was a penalty to be paid for the sin of man, and Jesus paid the penalty through His sacrifice. This met God's requirements for justice and allows Him to extend mercy to undeserving sinners.

As Christ died for sinners, He demonstrated God's righteousness, displayed His justice, and made His mercy possible.

As Paul says in Romans 3:23-26, "For all have sinned and fall short of the glory of God, [24] being justified as a gift by His grace through the redemption which is in Christ Jesus; [25] whom God displayed publicly as a propitiation in His blood through faith. This was to demonstrate His righteousness, because in the forbearance of God He passed over the sins previously committed; [26] for the demonstration, I say, of His righteousness at the present time, so that He would be just and the justifier of the one who has faith in Jesus."

God would never be unrighteous or unjust, not even to save man. God's justice demanded a price be paid. God extended His mercy by letting Jesus pay the price that satisfied the penalty.

Let us close with this thought: "But let justice roll down like waters And righteousness like an ever-flowing stream" (Amos 5:24).

Suggestions for further study: Find other scriptures that speak of the righteousness, justice, and mercy of God.

Daily Justice and Righteousness

Psalm 7:11 God is a righteous judge, And a God who has indignation every day.
Psalm 33:5 He loves righteousness and justice; The earth is full of the lovingkindness of the LORD.
Psalm 37:28 For the LORD loves justice And does not forsake His godly ones; They are preserved forever, But the descendants of the wicked will be cut off.
Psalm 71:19 For Your righteousness, O God, reaches to the heavens, You who have done great things; O God, who is like You?
Psalm 89:14 Righteousness and justice are the foundation of Your throne; Lovingkindness and truth go before You.
Psalm 116:5 Gracious is the LORD, and righteous; Yes, our God is compassionate.

39

Our Lord Who Remembers
and Remembers Not

Remember, O LORD, Your compassion and Your
lovingkindnesses, For they have been from of old.
⁷Do not remember the sins of my youth or my transgressions;
According to Your lovingkindness remember me,
For Your goodness' sake, O LORD.
Psalm 25:6-7

Just as in English, words in Hebrew often encompass multiple meanings and a range of ideas. People that study Hebrew tell us that the verbs often include not only mental processes but also the physical outcome or expected activity related to the mental process. An example is "hear" that we previously studied. "Remember" is another example. When the Bible says God "remembered," the original Hebrew verb is "zakar," which means "to remember and act on one's behalf."

The biblical examples of "remember" meaning "action on one's behalf" are numerous. When God "remembered" Noah, He made a wind blow over the earth, and the waters subsided (Genesis 8:1). When God "remembered" Rachel, God opened her womb and gave her a son (Genesis 30:22). When Joseph prophesied that Pharaoh's cupbearer would be restored from prison to his previous position, he asked the cupbearer to mention him to Pharaoh (Genesis 40:14). "Mention" in this verse is the same Hebrew word, "zakar," as in, "remember me to Pharaoh" so that he would release Joseph from prison.

When the Psalmist in Psalm 106:4 calls out, "Remember me, O LORD, in Your favor toward Your people; Visit me with Your salvation," the cry is not that God has forgotten that the Psalmist exists, rather it is a cry for God to turn His attention toward the Psalmist and rescue him from his situation.

Similarly, in Jeremiah 31:34, when God describes the new covenant, He says "For I will forgive their iniquity, and their sin I will remember no more." Here, God is not promising to forget our sin, but rather not to act in accordance with what it deserves. He is "not remembering" in the very Hebrew sense of not punishing us for our sin. Thank God for Psalm 103:12, "As far as the east is from the west, So far has He removed our transgressions from us."

Ecclesiastes 12:1 says, "Remember also your Creator in the days of your youth, before the evil days come and the years draw near when you will say, 'I have no delight in them.'" This is not just a mental activity to remember that God exists, but it is a call to "remember" the Lord in devotion to Him. Likewise, when the Israelites were instructed to "remember" the Sabbath Day, this meant that they were not just to think about it but were to observe it as God had decreed.

We can be so thankful that God does remember us, has turned His attention to us, and has acted upon our behalf by sending His Son. Because of His Son, our sins He will "remember no more."

Suggestions for further study: Do a word search for "remember." Can you find other examples of "remember" where it is indicating action?

Daily Remembering

Psalm 98:3 He has remembered His lovingkindness and His faithfulness to the house of Israel; All the ends of the earth have seen the salvation of our God.
Psalm 103:18 To those who keep His covenant And remember His precepts to do them.
Psalm 119:52 I have remembered Your ordinances from of old, O LORD, And comfort myself.
Psalm 119:55 O LORD, I remember Your name in the night, And keep Your law.

40

The Lord Abides Forever

But the LORD abides forever;
He has established His throne for judgment.
Psalm 9:7

"Forever" or even "forever and ever" in the scriptures do not always mean "for eternity" or "time without end." Rather, these terms signify "for as long as the conditions exist," which means the context must dictate the time frame meant.

For instance, look at Jonah 2:5-6 as Jonah prayed from the belly of the great fish: "Water encompassed me to the point of death. The great deep engulfed me, Weeds were wrapped around my head. 6I descended to the roots of the mountains. The earth with its bars was around me **forever**, But You have brought up my life from the pit, O LORD my God." We know that "forever" does not mean "time without end" because Jonah was in the fish's belly for only three days.

In several passages, the Psalmist uses the word "forever" to indicate the severity of being away from God. Psalm 77:7-8 says, "Will the Lord reject forever? And will He never be favorable again? Has His lovingkindness ceased forever? Has His promise come to an end forever?" It is similar to Jonah's lament. Jonah was not in the belly of the fish forever; it just felt like it.

In the same way, they use "forever" to indicate the bountiful blessings of the Lord. Psalm 21:4: "He asked life of You, You gave it to him, Length of days forever and ever." David is speaking of himself here—that the Lord had blessed him with many days. They also speak of worshipping God forever. Psalms 86:12 I will give thanks to You, O Lord my God, with all my heart, And will glorify Your name forever."

When speaking of God, "forever and ever" can mean eternal, without beginning or end. For example:

Psalm 10:16 The LORD is King forever and ever; Nations have perished from His land.

Psalm 45:6 Your throne, O God, is forever and ever; A scepter of uprightness is the scepter of Your kingdom.

Psalm 90:2 Before the mountains were born Or You gave birth to the earth and the world, Even from everlasting to everlasting, You are God.

Psalm 92:8 But You, O LORD, are on high forever.

Psalm 102:12 But You, O LORD, abide forever, And Your name to all generations.

Psalm 117:2 For His lovingkindness is great toward us, And the truth of the LORD is everlasting. Praise the LORD!

The lesson for us is that God is not constrained by time, but we are. Psalm 103:15-17: "As for man, his days are like grass; As a flower of the field, so he flourishes. [16]When the wind has passed over it, it is no more, And its place acknowledges it no longer. [17]But the lovingkindness of the LORD is from everlasting to everlasting on those who fear Him, And His righteousness to children's children." The writers of this book are in their seventies. You may think that we have lived a long time, but no, it has been just as the lifespan of a flower in the field, soon to be blown away.

Suggestions for further study: Let us consider our lives; they are just a vapor. Are we preparing every day to meet our eternal Father in judgment? Find scriptures related to the brevity of life.

Daily Reading of Time and Eternity

Psalm 19:9 The fear of the LORD is clean, enduring forever; The judgments of the LORD are true; they are righteous altogether.

Psalm 23:6 Surely goodness and lovingkindness will follow me all the days of my life, And I will dwell in the house of the LORD forever.

Psalm 33:11 The counsel of the LORD stands forever, The plans of His heart from generation to generation.

Psalm 89:52 Blessed be the LORD forever! Amen and Amen.

LESSON XI

Praise God from Whom All Blessings Flow

NOTES

41

In the Assembly

Praise the LORD! I will give thanks to the LORD with all my heart,
In the company of the upright and in the assembly.
Psalm 111:1

In Psalm 22:22 it says, "I will tell of Your name to my brethren; In the midst of the assembly I will praise You." Our public assembly is very important to us; indeed, it is essential to our spiritual strength. Recent challenges to our in-person public gatherings have shown us that nothing can substitute for the blessings that we receive when we assemble in the same place, at the same time, to pour out our hearts to God together with beloved brothers and sisters.

Church gatherings are not the invention of man. The Lord Himself ordained these opportunities for us to fellowship with one another in our worship. The church began assembling immediately after its inception. Acts 2:42-47 says, "They were continually devoting themselves to the apostles' teaching and to fellowship, to the breaking of bread and to prayer. 43Everyone kept feeling a sense of awe; and many wonders and signs were taking place through the apostles. 44And all those who had believed were together and had all things in common; 45and they began selling their property and possessions and were sharing them with all, as anyone might have need. 46Day by day continuing with one mind in the temple, and breaking bread from house to house, they were taking their meals together with gladness and sincerity of heart, 47praising God and having favor with all the people. And the Lord was adding to their number day by day those who were being saved." In the context of encouraging the brethren to remain strong in the Lord, Hebrews 10:25 gives a sincere warning against abandoning the assembling.

The Lord has devised the greatest support group ever made. He made us and knows us, and knows what we need. Let us thank God for His gift, a loving company of the upright. Look at some of the many "one anothers" that the Lord provides for us in the church.

Daily Reading: How We Treat One Another in the Church

Romans 12:10 Be devoted to one another in brotherly love; give preference to one another in honor.

Romans 12:16a Be of the same mind toward one another; do not be haughty in mind, but associate with the lowly.

Romans 14:19 So then we pursue the things which make for peace and the building up of one another.

Romans 15:7 Therefore, accept one another, just as Christ also accepted us to the glory of God.

2 Corinthians 13:12 Greet one another with a holy kiss.

Galatians 6:2a Bear one another's burdens.

Ephesians 4:2 With all humility and gentleness, with patience, showing tolerance for one another in love.

Ephesians 4:32 Be kind to one another, tender-hearted, forgiving each other, just as God in Christ also has forgiven you.

Philippians 2:3 Do nothing from selfishness or empty conceit, but with humility of mind regard one another as more important than yourselves.

1 Thessalonians 5:11 Therefore encourage one another and build up one another, just as you also are doing.

Hebrews 3:13 But encourage one another day after day, as long as it is still called "Today," so that none of you will be hardened by the deceitfulness of sin.

Hebrews 10:24-25 And let us consider how to stimulate one another to love and good deeds, [25]not forsaking our own assembling together, as is the habit of some, but encouraging one another; and all the more as you see the day drawing near.

James 5:16a Therefore, confess your sins to one another, and pray for one another so that you may be healed.

1 Peter 1:22 Since you have in obedience to the truth purified your souls for a sincere love of the brethren, fervently love one another from the heart.

1 John 3:11 For this is the message which you have heard from the beginning, that we should love one another.

42

O How Love I the Law

The Law of the LORD is perfect, restoring the soul; The testimony
of the LORD is sure, making wise the simple. ⁸The precepts of
the LORD are right, rejoicing the heart; The commandment of
the LORD is pure, enlightening the eyes. ⁹The fear of the LORD is
clean, enduring forever; The judgments of the LORD are true; they
are righteous altogether. ¹⁰They are more desirable than gold, yes,
than much fine gold; Sweeter also than honey and drippings of the
honeycomb. ¹¹Moreover, by them Your servant is warned;
In keeping them there is great reward.
Psalms 19:7-11

The Psalmists clearly loved the law of God, as we should. And
even more so, because with the coming of Christ, a grand purpose
of the law is revealed. Romans 10:4: "For Christ is the end [or
culmination] of the law for righteousness to everyone who
believes."

Galatians 3:24: "Therefore the Law has become our tutor to
lead us to Christ, so that we may be justified by faith." John 5:39
says, "You search the Scriptures because you think that in them you
have eternal life; it is these that testify about Me."

Let us thank God for the Law and for Jesus Christ who fulfilled
it. We are blessed to know what the people of old did not. You
know how sometimes when you see a movie for the second time,
you notice things and realize nuances that you didn't when you saw
it the first time? Well, that is how I picture us reading the Old
Testament. Imagine living then and hearing a prophecy. How about
Isaiah 7:14, which states: "Therefore the Lord Himself will give you
a sign: Behold, a virgin will be with child and bear a son, and she
will call His name Immanuel"? Imagine how perplexing that would

have been, but we are blessed with the understanding that Jesus fulfilled it. He fulfilled it all.

Instead of obeying the Old Testament Law, Christians today are to obey the law of Christ found in the New Testament. 1 John 5:3 declares, "For this is the love of God, that we keep His commandments; and His commandments are not burdensome." The apostle Paul says, "What then? Shall we sin because we are not under law but under grace? May it never be!" (Romans 6:15).

Love is to be our motivation to obey God's commands. When we recognize the value of Jesus' sacrifice on our behalf, our response is love, gratitude, and obedience to the law of Christ and to the Lawgiver. Can we claim to love the Lawgiver and not love His law?

Suggestions for further study: Read Psalm 119 and note all the examples of attitude toward the law.

Daily Love of the Law

Psalm 1:1-2 How blessed is the man who does not walk in the counsel of the wicked, Nor stand in the path of sinners, Nor sit in the seat of scoffers! ²But his delight is in the law of the LORD, And in His law he meditates day and night.

Psalm 37:31 The law of his God is in his heart; His steps do not slip.

Psalm 40:8 I delight to do Your will, O my God; Your Law is within my heart."

Psalm 94:12 Blessed is the man whom You chasten, O LORD, And whom You teach out of Your law.

Psalm 119:34 Give me understanding, that I may observe Your law And keep it with all my heart.

Psalm 119:165 Those who love Your law have great peace, And nothing causes them to stumble.

Psalm 119:174 I long for Your salvation, O LORD, And Your law is my delight.

43

God the Lawgiver

I delight to do Your will, O my God; Your Law is within my heart.
Psalm 40:8

In the last section, we studied about loving God's law. Now we emphasize the Lawgiver. Since many of the characteristics of the law correspond to characteristics of God, we could think of the law as a mirror of God's character. For instance, God is love and His law is an expression of His love. We would not even know love without it. Likewise, God is righteous, and His law is an expression of His righteousness. We cannot be righteous without it. It is holy like He is holy, and likewise we cannot be holy without it. Trying to have a relationship with God without keeping His law is futile.

The Psalmists make it clear that they saw it that way. They described God's law in very positive terms. I hear people sometimes say, "I'm glad that I don't have to be under the old law and do all that stuff today." And I guess in hindsight under our "better" law, we can feel that way. But the Psalmists did not regret being under the law of God. Loving the Lawgiver makes loving the law possible. Loving the Lawgiver makes obedience to Him and His law pleasant.

We are bound by the law of Christ today rather than the law of Moses as the Psalmists were, but aren't we glad that we have it "for our instruction" (Romans 15:4)? How shallow would be our understanding of the law of Christ without the Old Testament. Let us look at just one of many, many examples. When John the Baptist saw Jesus coming toward Him (John 1:29), he said, "Behold, the Lamb of God, who takes away the sins of the world!" making a profound prophecy of what Jesus would do for all mankind. But think of how little we would understand about that without the many references to sacrificial lambs of the Old Testament.

We know that all the scriptures, both Old and New Testaments, are the inspired word of God and contain God's law. We tend to use phrases like the "law of God" and "word of God" interchangeably, and from Psalm 119, it appears that the Psalmists did likewise. 2 Timothy 3:16-17 says, "All Scripture is inspired by God and profitable for teaching, for reproof, for correction, for training in righteousness; [17]so that the man of God may be adequate, equipped for every good work."

Without the law, or the word, it would be impossible for us to know God. That He would let us know Him is an honor and privilege to us. The Lord Himself said in Jeremiah 9:23-24, "Let not a wise man boast of his wisdom, and let not the mighty man boast of his might, let not a rich man boast of his riches; [24]but let him who boasts boast of this, that he understands and knows Me, that I am the LORD who exercises lovingkindness, justice and righteousness on earth; for I delight in these things." Having a relationship with God and truly knowing Him is something that is worth boasting about.

If we do not see the law as the Psalmists saw it, as a delight, then maybe we need to pray as in Psalm 119:18: "Open my eyes that I may behold Wonderful things from your law." We need to thank God for His word. Imagine your life without the law of God. A life without the law would be a life without the Lawgiver.

Suggestions for further study: Below are more verses about the law. As we reflect on them, let us think about what they tell us about the relationship between the Psalmist and the Lawgiver.

Daily Love of the Lawgiver

Psalm 94:12 Blessed is the man whom You chasten, O LORD, And whom You teach out of Your law.
Psalm 105:45 So that they might keep His statutes And observe His laws, Praise the LORD!
Psalm 119:1 How blessed are those whose way is blameless, Who walk in the law of the LORD.
Psalm 119:10 With all my heart I have sought You; Do not let me wander from Your commandments.

44

Teach Me Your Way

Teach me Your way, O LORD; I will walk in Your truth;
Unite my heart to fear Your name.
Psalm 86:11

Consider David's stature – the king of Israel, ruler over a great nation, and yet as you read the Psalms, he is forever asking God to teach Him. We seldom see business and industry or government leaders who desire knowledge of God. Imagine a U.S. President who would say like King David said in Psalm 25:4-5, "Make me know Your ways, O LORD; Teach me Your paths. Lead me in Your truth and teach me, For You are the God of my salvation; For You I wait all the day."

David was a wise man, as depicted by Solomon in Proverbs 1:5: "A wise man will hear and increase in learning, And a man of understanding will acquire wise counsel." David knew God, but that did not stop him from continuing to ask for Him to "teach me."

The lesson for us: however much we know about God and His word, our prayer should be, "teach me your way." No preacher or elder knows so much that he should not humbly say, "teach me." No one does. And this teaching is first for our own heart's sake. In Ezra 7:10, Ezra had "set his heart to study the law of the LORD and to practice it, and to teach His statutes and ordinances in Israel." Our study must never become centered solely on what others need. First and foremost, teach *ME* your paths.

David also sought to teach God's will to others. In his prayer of repentance in Psalm 51:12-13, he promises, "Restore to me the joy of Your salvation And sustain me with a willing spirit. [13]Then I will teach transgressors Your ways, And sinners will be converted to

You." Another lesson for us: We must purify our own hearts so that we can teach others. We need to be an example before others will listen to us. Also, we must show love. They won't care what we know until they know that we care.

An example of David's teaching is found in Psalm 34:11-14: "Come, you children, listen to me; I will teach you the fear of the LORD. [12]Who is the man who desires life And loves length of days that he may see good? [13]Keep your tongue from evil And your lips from speaking deceit.[14]Depart from evil and do good; Seek peace and pursue it."

Suggestions for further study Psalm 78:4-6 speaks of teaching our children. It is referring to Deuteronomy 6 and 11. Verse six says, "That the generation to come might know, even the children yet to be born, That they may arise and tell them to their children." We all must take the teaching of our children more seriously, not just in a set Bible study time but all through the day, every day. Pray for the teaching of our children. Grandparents, let us teach our grandchildren to know God. Let them hear us everyday praise God and see us obey His will. It is the best way to teach them.

Daily Teaching

Psalm 119:12 Blessed are You, O LORD; Teach me Your statutes.
Psalm 119:26 I have told of my ways, and You have answered me; Teach me Your statutes.
Psalm 119:33 Teach me, O LORD, the way of Your statutes, And I shall observe it to the end.
Psalm 119:64 The earth is full of Your lovingkindness, O LORD; Teach me Your statutes.
Psalm 119:66 Teach me good discernment and knowledge, For I believe in Your commandments.
Psalm 119:68 You are good and do good; Teach me Your statutes.
Psalm 119:99 I have more insight than all my teachers, For Your testimonies are my meditation.
Psalm 119:108 O accept the freewill offerings of my mouth, O LORD, And teach me Your ordinances.

LESSON XII

O To Be Like Thee

NOTES

45

Today If You Would
Hear His Voice

For He is our God, And we are the people of His pasture and the
sheep of His hand. Today, if you would hear His voice,
[8]Do not harden your hearts.
Psalm 95:7-8a

Don't we all have loved ones of whom we would say, "if you
only would hear His voice." In this Psalm the Psalmist is inviting
others to come and worship with him. As you read, notice the
entreaties to "come let us" worship.

Psalm 95:1-7a: "O come, let us sing for joy to the LORD, Let
us shout joyfully to the rock of our salvation. [2] Let us come before
His presence with thanksgiving, Let us shout joyfully to Him with
psalms. [3] For the LORD is a great God And a great King above all
gods, [4] In whose hand are the depths of the earth, The peaks of the
mountains are His also. [5]The sea is His, for it was He who made it,
And His hands formed the dry land. [6]Come, let us worship and bow
down, Let us kneel before the LORD our Maker. [7]For He is our
God, And we are the people of His pasture and the sheep of His
hand."

Then the Psalmist utters the great words, "Today, if you would
hear His voice, Do not harden your hearts" (Psalm 95:7b-8a). In
Matthew 7:24, Jesus said, "Therefore everyone who hears these
words of Mine and acts on them, may be compared to a wise man
who built his house on the rock." But alas, in Matthew 7:26, Jesus
continued, "Everyone who hears these words of Mine and does not
act on them, will be like a foolish man who built his house on the
sand." We must not harden our hearts against the voice of God. If
we do, what hope do we have? Since the scripture says, "Do not

harden your hearts," that means it is in our control. It is up to us. We can hear the voice of God and His word with a tender, obedient heart, if we will.

Not everyone would follow Jesus, hear His words, and act on them—not then and not now. All we can do is offer His invitation. Matthew 11:28-30: "Come to Me, all who are weary and heavy-laden, and I will give you rest. [29] Take My yoke upon you and learn from Me, for I am gentle and humble in heart, and you will find rest for your souls. [30] For My yoke is easy and My burden is light."

We can be an invitation to others to come with us. Matthew 5:14-16: "You are the light of the world. A city set on a hill cannot be hidden; [15]nor does anyone light a lamp and put it under a basket, but on the lampstand, and it gives light to all who are in the house. [16] Let your light shine before men in such a way that they may see your good works, and glorify your Father who is in heaven."

The refrain of *On Jordan's Stormy Banks* (by Alfred G. Karnes) captures this invitation:

I am bound for the promised land,
I am bound for the promised land;
Oh, who will come and go with me?
I am bound for the promised land.

Suggestions for further study: Find hymns that are invitations to follow Jesus. Let us look for ways to be a light to others and to say, "Oh, who will come and go with me? I am bound for the promised land."

Daily Invitation

Psalm 34:3 O magnify the LORD with me, And let us exalt His name together.
Psalm 118:24 This is the day which the LORD has made; Let us rejoice and be glad in it.
Psalm 122:1 I was glad when they said to me, "Let us go to the house of the LORD."
Psalm 132:7 Let us go into His dwelling place; Let us worship at His footstool.

46

Draw Near to God

But as for me, the nearness of God is my good; I have made the
Lord GOD my refuge, That I may tell of all Your works.
Psalm 73:28

Psalm 128:1 says, "How blessed is everyone who fears the
LORD, Who walks in His ways." This is the "happy" meaning of
the word "blessed." It is a satisfying, blessed way to live, as
conveyed in the prayer hymn, *Nearer Still Nearer* (by Lelia N.
Morris).

Nearer, still nearer, close to Thy heart,
Draw me, my Savior—so precious Thou art!
Fold me, oh, fold me close to Thy breast;
Shelter me safe in that "haven of rest;"
Shelter me safe in that "haven of rest."

Nearer, still nearer, nothing I bring,
Naught as an off'ring to Jesus, my King;
Only my sinful, now contrite heart,
Grant me the cleansing Thy blood doth impart;
Grant me the cleansing Thy blood doth impart.

Nearer, still nearer, Lord, to be Thine!
Sin, with its follies, I gladly resign,
All of its pleasures, pomp and its pride,
Give me but Jesus, my Lord crucified;
Give me but Jesus, my Lord crucified.

Nearer, still nearer, while life shall last,
Till safe in glory my anchor is cast;
Through endless ages ever to be
Nearer, my Savior, still nearer to Thee;
Nearer, my Savior, still nearer to Thee!

Coming near to God is a theme throughout the scriptures. James 4:8a says, "Draw near to God and He will draw near to you." When describing the priesthood of Jesus, the Hebrew writer describes those that Jesus will save in Hebrews 7:25: "Therefore He is able also to save forever those who draw near to God through Him, since He always lives to make intercession for them."

Indeed, in several places, Hebrews emphasizes drawing near to God:

Hebrews 4:16 Therefore let us draw near with confidence to the throne of grace, so that we may receive mercy and find grace to help in time of need.

Hebrews 7:19 (For the Law made nothing perfect), and on the other hand there is a bringing in of a better hope, through which we draw near to God.

Hebrews 10:22 Let us draw near with a sincere heart in full assurance of faith, having our hearts sprinkled clean from an evil conscience and our bodies washed with pure water.

Suggestions for further study: Find other hymns and scriptures that encourage drawing near to God.

Daily Nearness to God

Psalm 34:18 The LORD is near to the brokenhearted And saves those who are crushed in spirit.

Psalm 65:4 How blessed is the one whom You choose and bring near to You To dwell in Your courts. We will be satisfied with the goodness of Your house, Your holy temple.

Psalm 69:18 Oh draw near to my soul and redeem it; Ransom me because of my enemies!

Psalm 75:1 We give thanks to You, O God, we give thanks, For Your name is near; Men declare Your wondrous works.

Psalm 145:18 The LORD is near to all who call upon Him, To all who call upon Him in truth.

Psalm 148:14 And He has lifted up a horn for His people, Praise for all His godly ones; Even for the sons of Israel, a people near to Him. Praise the LORD!

47

Seek the Lord

O God, You are my God; I shall seek You earnestly;
My soul thirsts for You, my flesh yearns for You,
In a dry and weary land where there is no water.
Psalm 63:1

Hebrews 11:6 tells us, "And without faith it is impossible to please Him, for he who comes to God must believe that He is and that He is a rewarder of those who seek Him." It is hard to imagine a more diligent seeker of God than David in the focus verse above. We picture a man, this "man after God's own heart," seeking God like a thirsty man in the desert seeks water.

When David speaks of seeking God, he frequently emphasizes this diligence. Psalm 105:4: "Seek the LORD and His strength; Seek His face continually." Psalm 119:2: "How blessed are those who observe His testimonies, Who seek Him with all their heart."

Contrast this with the haughty and wicked man who will not seek God. Psalm 10:4: "The wicked, in the haughtiness of his countenance, does not seek Him. All his thoughts are, 'There is no God.'"

Psalm 27:4: "One thing I have asked from the LORD, that I shall seek: That I may dwell in the house of the LORD all the days of my life, To behold the beauty of the LORD And to meditate in His temple." We know that David requested other things from the Lord, but he seemed to be asserting that this was the most important thing. All other requests paled in comparison to this.

In Psalm 83:1-2, David prays, "O God, do not remain quiet; Do not be silent and, O God, do not be still. ²For behold, Your enemies make an uproar, And those who hate You have exalted themselves." Then in verse sixteen, he prays, "Fill their faces with dishonor, That they may seek Your name, O LORD."

David asks for "dishonor" to come on God's enemies so that they might seek God. Calamity in our lives may turn us to God. In the vernacular of our day, we say, "Sometimes you must hit rock bottom." In the story of the prodigal son in Luke 15, he had to wake up in the pigpen before resolving to return to his father.

Why would we needlessly subject ourselves to this kind of pain? Seeking God is liberty: "And I will walk at liberty, For I seek Your precepts" (Psalm 119:45). And seeking God is joy: "Let all who seek You rejoice and be glad in You; And let those who love Your salvation say continually, 'Let God be magnified'" (Psalm 70:4). And Psalm 105:3 says, "Glory in His holy name; Let the heart of those who seek the LORD be glad."

Suggestions for further study: Contrast the idea of seeking self or seeking God. How can we move from one to the other?

Daily Seek the Lord

Psalm 9:10 And those who know Your name will put their trust in You, For You, O LORD, have not forsaken those who seek You.
Psalm 22:26 The afflicted will eat and be satisfied; Those who seek Him will praise the LORD. Let your heart live forever!
Psalm 105:3 Glory in His holy name; Let the heart of those who seek the LORD be glad.
Psalm 105:4 Seek the LORD and His strength; Seek His face continually.

48

Try My Heart

You have tried my heart; You have visited me by night;
You have tested me and You find nothing;
I have purposed that my mouth will not transgress.
Psalm 17:3

"Heart" is found 127 times in the Psalms (NASB1995) with different meanings. The scriptures use the word "heart" primarily to refer to the core of our being. It is the center of our will, intellect and emotions.

"Heart" sometimes means the mind as in Psalm 4:4, where David offers advice, perhaps to soldiers in wartimes. "Tremble, and do not sin; Meditate in your heart upon your bed, and be still. *Selah*." Sometimes it is the seat of emotions, as in Psalm 4:7, where he says, "You have put gladness in my heart."

Sometimes "heart" signifies the moral seat of man that is judged. Psalm 7:9 says, "For the righteous God tries the hearts and minds. "Heart's desire" is an expression that means something wanted very much. Psalm 10:3 states, "For the wicked boasts of his heart's desire."

"All my heart" or "whole heart" emphasizes the extent of commitment and devotion. Psalm 9:1: "I will give thanks to the LORD with all my heart; I will tell of all Your wonders." This is the kind of whole-hearted service that God wants from us.

When David said in Psalm 17:3, "You have tried my heart; You have visited me by night; You have tested me and You find nothing; I have purposed that my mouth will not transgress," he speaks of the Lord trying our hearts. We must learn to try our own hearts as well. "Trying our hearts" means to examine or scrutinize our lives, taking an intense look at our spiritual beings. This is not always a pleasant exercise. It takes an honest assessment of our commitment to the Lord. Is it really our "constant longing and prayer" to be like the Lord?

God does not want us to just skip along on the path of life, giving little thought to our relationship with Him. Psalm 119:59 says, "I considered my ways And turned my feet to Your testimonies." Paul says in 2 Corinthians 13:5: "Test yourselves to see if you are in the faith; examine yourselves! Or do you not recognize this about yourselves, that Jesus Christ is in you—unless indeed you fail the test?" Part of our walk with the Lord is examining our hearts, testing them by the testimonies of the Lord, and then praying for strength to cleanse and strengthen them.

Suggestions for further study: Remember, "heart" occurs 127 times in Psalms. Do a word search to discover other examples, and as you read, stop and think about how it is being used. *Selah.*

Daily Heart Strengthening

Psalm 7:9 O let the evil of the wicked come to an end, but establish the righteous; For the righteous God tries the hearts and minds.
Psalm 13:5 But I have trusted in Your lovingkindness; My heart shall rejoice in Your salvation.
Psalm 14:1 The fool has said in his heart, "There is no God." They are corrupt, they have committed abominable deeds; There is no one who does good.
Psalm 15:2 He who walks with integrity, and works righteousness, And speaks truth in his heart.
Psalm 16:9 Therefore my heart is glad and my glory rejoices; My flesh also will dwell securely.
Psalm 49:3 My mouth will speak wisdom, And the meditation of my heart will be understanding.
Psalm 139:23-24 Search me, O God, and know my heart; Try me and know my anxious thoughts; [24]And see if there be any hurtful way in me, And lead me in the everlasting way.

LESSON XIII

It is Well With My Soul

NOTES

49

Lead Me in Your Truth

Make me know Your ways, O LORD; Teach me Your paths.
⁵Lead me in Your truth and teach me,
For You are the God of my salvation; For You I wait all the day.
Psalm 25:4-5

Our lives must be centered on following God's paths. Psalm 40:8 says, "I delight to do Your will, O my God; Your Law is within my heart." We began this study in Lesson One with praising God. From the Psalms, we gain appreciation for the deep devotion of heart that the Psalmists offered to the Lord. Yet consider the warning of Jesus to the Pharisees. Matthew 15:7-9: "You hypocrites, rightly did Isaiah prophesy of you: ⁸'This people honors Me with their lips, But their heart is far away from Me. ⁹But in vain do they worship Me, Teaching as doctrines the precepts of men.'"

Samuel asked King Saul in 1 Samuel 15:22: "Has the LORD as much delight in burnt offerings and sacrifices As in obeying the voice of the LORD?" And then gave the answer: "Behold, to obey is better than sacrifice, And to heed than the fat of rams."

Obedience is a fundamental element of our relationship with God. Praise without obedience is merely flattery. Think of a defiant, disobedient child telling his parents how wonderful they are. It is empty praise. But the prayer in Psalm 143:10 describes why we long to do the will of God: "Teach me to do Your will, For You are my God; Let Your good Spirit lead me on level ground." Why should we do the will of God? Because He is our God. It is fundamental to the relationship. The Psalmist also prayed, "Let Your good Spirit lead me."

Psalm 119:105 tells us that God leads through His word: "Your word is a lamp to my feet And a light to my path." Psalm 48:14

describes the guidance of the Lord: "For such is God, Our God forever and ever; He will guide us until death." And the most beloved of Psalms says, "He makes me lie down in green pastures; He leads me beside quiet waters…He guides me in the paths of righteousness For His name's sake" (Psalm 23:2, 3b). God has not left us stranded out in the cold. This care and guidance of sheep illustrates the spiritual care and guidance that we get from the Lord. Now there is only one thing left—we must follow. If the sheep willfully or carelessly wander off from the shepherd's care, his care and guidance is of no value.

Psalm 33:1 says, "Sing for joy in the LORD, O you righteous ones; Praise is becoming to the upright." We might say a hat is becoming; it suits us. We look good in it. That's how praise is on the upright. The upright cannot praise God too long or too loudly. It sounds good on them. So let us determine to be of the upright.

Suggestions for further study: Find hymns about leading and following.

Daily Leading and Following

Psalm 5:8 O LORD, lead me in Your righteousness because of my foes; Make Your way straight before me.
Psalm 23:2 He makes me lie down in green pastures; He leads me beside quiet waters.
Psalm 25:5 Lead me in Your truth and teach me, For You are the God of my salvation; For You I wait all the day.
Psalm 31:3 For You are my rock and my fortress; For Your name's sake You will lead me and guide me.
Psalm 38:20 And those who repay evil for good, They oppose me, because I follow what is good.
Psalm 43:3 O send out Your light and Your truth, let them lead me; Let them bring me to Your holy hill And to Your dwelling places.
Psalm 61:2 From the end of the earth I call to You when my heart is faint; Lead me to the rock that is higher than I.
Psalm 139:24 And see if there be any hurtful way in me, And lead me in the everlasting way.

50

What Is Man That You Take Thought of Him?

What is man that You take thought of him, And the
son of man that You care for him?
Psalm 8:4

This is one of the most profound questions ever posed. David raises it twice in the Psalms: here in Psalm 8 and again in Psalm 144:3.

Notice the context of the question in chapter 8: "When I consider Your heavens, the work of Your fingers, The moon and the stars, which You have ordained; 4What is man that You take thought of him, And the son of man that You care for him? 5Yet You have made him a little lower than God, And You crown him with glory and majesty! 6You make him to rule over the works of Your hands; You have put all things under his feet, 7All sheep and oxen, And also the beasts of the field, 8The birds of the heavens and the fish of the sea, Whatever passes through the paths of the seas." (Psalm 8:3-8).

You can almost picture David shaking his head in amazement when he observed the beauties of the night sky and proclaimed, "O LORD, our Lord, How majestic is Your name in all the earth!" (Psalm 8:9). Why would such a magnificent Creator care about lowly man? In comparison to God and to His majesty, man seems utterly unworthy to be esteemed by such a great God. Surely, we have all felt just like David. We may think, "How could you love me enough to give up your Son, Oh God? I am nothing."

In the context of Hebrews 2:6-18, the writer quotes this Psalm to show us that Jesus humbled himself and became a man. As a man, He was "for a little while lower than the angels" (verse 7). As a man, He willingly experienced suffering and death, just as we do. Verses 17-18 say, "Therefore, He had to be made like His brethren in all things, so that He might become a merciful and faithful high priest in things pertaining to God, to make propitiation for the sins of the people. [18]For since He Himself was tempted in that which He has suffered, He is able to come to the aid of those who are tempted." Therefore, when you ask the question, "What is man?" the greatest answer is: the one that Jesus willingly left heaven to become and the one for whom Jesus was willing to die.

"What is man?" Man is the one that God made in His image and loves with such mercy. Psalm 103:11,14: "For as high as the heavens are above the earth, So great is His lovingkindness toward those who fear Him." [14]"For He Himself knows our frame; He is mindful that we are but dust." Thanks be to God that despite man's lowliness and God's greatness, He loves and cares for us. That is what we are.

Suggestions for further study: Write your own answer to the question, "What is man?"

Daily Recognition of Jesus as Man

Philippians 2:5-8 Have this attitude in yourselves which was also in Christ Jesus, [6]who, although He existed in the form of God, did not regard equality with God a thing to be grasped, [7]but emptied Himself, taking the form of a bond-servant, and being made in the likeness of men. [8]Being found in appearance as a man, He humbled Himself by becoming obedient to the point of death, even death on a cross.

Hebrews 5:8-9 Although He was a Son, He learned obedience from the things which He suffered. [9]And having been made perfect, He became to all those who obey Him the source of eternal salvation.

John 1:14 And the Word became flesh, and dwelt among us, and we saw His glory, glory as of the only begotten from the Father, full of grace and truth.

51

Longing for God's Presence

Surely the righteous will give thanks to Your name;
The upright will dwell in Your presence.
Psalm 140:13

Truth of eternal life is revealed much more thoroughly and explicitly in the New Testament than in the Old, although there are shadows of it in the Old, including in the Psalms. By the time of Jesus, there was a widespread belief in the resurrection of the dead, though it was not universally accepted (the Sadducees being one exception). This knowledge had to have come from the Old Testament. Even in the New Testament we get only glimpses of what heaven is like, not a detailed picture. Perhaps this is because we cannot know the wonders of heaven with our finite minds. But there is only one thing that we need to know about it to know that we want to go there—God is there.

"Sheol," or grave, is found fifteen times in Psalms; some are prophecies of Jesus. In Psalm 16:10, David foretells the resurrection of the Lord: "For You will not abandon my soul to Sheol; Nor will You allow Your Holy One to undergo decay," and the prophecy is quoted both in Acts 2 and 13 to show that it was Jesus of whom he spoke.

Let us look at two other references. The first is Psalms 49:15: "But God will redeem my soul from the power of Sheol, For He will receive me. *Selah*." A similar statement is made in Psalm 73:23-24, where the Psalmist first describes his walk with God: "Nevertheless I am continually with You; You have taken hold of my right hand. [24]With Your counsel You will guide me, And afterward receive me to glory." "Afterward" means "after death." The Psalmist says that after the walk here together, after death, God will "receive" him to glory.

Yearning for heaven is a natural extension of a close relationship with God. Are we, like the Psalmist, dwelling in His presence? Are we continually with Him? Do we let the Lord take our hand as we walk here together? Do we let His counsel guide us? That prepares us for being received into glory afterward.

Sometimes, people describe heaven as a glorified earth. "I know Uncle Billy is up there fishing with Peter," or, "Imagine what the golf courses in heaven are going to be like." Is that what heaven will be like? Remember, there is only one thing that we need to know about it to know that we want to go there—God is there.

God's glory will fill heaven. Our worship of Him and our relationship with Him will be more meaningful because we will not be hindered by any doubt or shame, or temptation, or the limits of a finite mind. We will be able to fully and freely give our hearts to God, to give and receive love. His glory will fill heaven, and all the righteous will dwell in His glorious presence. That is what heaven will be like.

Suggestions for further study: Think of your relationship with God. How would you describe it? Do you let God lead you by the hand, guiding you continually? Make a list of songs and scriptures that encourage us to walk closer with the Lord and that point our eyes to heaven.

Daily Dwelling in His Presence

Psalm 16:11 You will make known to me the path of life; In Your presence is fullness of joy; In Your right hand there are pleasures forever.
Psalm 95:2 Let us come before His presence with thanksgiving; Let us shout joyfully to Him with psalms.

52

Looking Forward

These are My words which I spoke to you while I was still with
you, that all things which are written about Me in the Law of Moses
and the Prophets and the Psalms must be fulfilled.
Luke 24:44

Well, we were not really prepared for what a rich study the
Psalms was going to be when we began it. A study of Psalms
engages the heart and mind in the loftiest of thoughts about the
Most Holy and Highest One. It also gives a great example of a close
relationship with the Lord. And just as importantly, it reveals the
deeply compelling eternal plans of God, pointing forward to the
coming of the Messiah. There are more references to Psalms in the
New Testament than to any other Old Testament book. We must
not take the Psalms lightly. They are not just flowery words to put
on greeting cards.

Shortly before his ascension, Jesus said to his disciples in Luke
24:44-47, "'These are My words which I spoke to you while I was
still with you, that all things which are written about Me in the Law
of Moses and the Prophets and the Psalms must be fulfilled.' [45]Then
He opened their minds to understand the Scriptures, [46]and He said
to them, 'Thus it is written, that the Christ would suffer and rise
again from the dead the third day, [47]and that repentance for
forgiveness of sins would be proclaimed in His name to all the
nations, beginning from Jerusalem.'"

The Psalms had been central to the Jews' worship of God for
centuries before Christ. Imagine how it would have been to live
your whole life singing those songs, and then one day finally
learning what they meant. Perhaps that familiarity is why the Holy
Spirit used the Psalms so extensively to prove that Jesus was the
promised Messiah. Consider a few examples. In Luke 1:46-55, Mary

quotes repeatedly from the Psalms in her song, as does Zacharias, the father of John the Baptist, in Luke 1:68-79. In Luke 4:10-11, while tempting Jesus, Satan misuses Psalm 91:11-12. Jesus used the Psalms more than any other Old Testament book. For instance, He quoted from Psalm 110:1, baffling the Pharisees (Matthew 22:44).

Peter used that same Psalm in Acts 2:34-35 in the Pentecost sermon to convince the people that the One that they had crucified is the promised Messiah. And the Hebrew writer used it in Hebrews 1:13 to show that Jesus is greater than the angels. In Acts 13, Paul refers to Psalm 2:7 and Psalm 16:10. Countless other examples permeate the rest of the New Testament. The Psalms played a major role in convincing the Jews that Jesus was the promised Messiah.

Our study of Psalms leaves us with a deep appreciation for its power and significance and of how shallow our understanding of it still is. God had a well-defined purpose for the Psalms. Nothing would help us more in our life with God than to start over studying the Psalms again. Use it as a prayer book, as many are prayers. Use it as a study book; there is so much history and prophecy in the book. Read through it over and over to get a broad overview of the majesty of God. However you choose to study them, we hope that you will continue your study of the great and glorious Psalms. Our study just whets the appetite for more.

Suggestions for further study: Research more of the quotations from Psalms in the New Testament.

We end this study with the last verse of the Psalms:

Psalm 150:6 Let everything that has breath praise the LORD. Praise the LORD!

Psalms Year-Long
Reading Schedule

Week 1: Psalms 1-3
Memory Verse: _____
Notes: _____

Week 2: Psalms 4-6
Memory Verse: _____
Notes: _____

Week 3: Psalms 7-9
Memory Verse: _____
Notes: _____

Week 4: Psalms 10-12
Memory Verse: _____
Notes: _____

Week 5: Psalms 13-15
Memory Verse: _____
Notes: _____

Week 6: Psalms 16-18
Memory Verse: _____
Notes: _____

Week 7: Psalms 19-21
Memory Verse: _____

Notes:_____

Week 8: Psalms 22-23
Memory Verse: _____
Notes:_____

Week 9: Psalms 24-26
Memory Verse: _____
Notes:_____

Week 10: Psalms 27-30
Memory Verse: _____
Notes:_____

Week 11: Psalms 31-32
Memory Verse: _____
Notes:_____

Week 12: Psalms 33-35
Memory Verse: _____
Notes:_____

Week 13: Psalms 36-38
Memory Verse: _____
Notes:_____

Week 14: Psalms 39-41
Memory Verse: _____
Notes:_____

Week 15: Psalms 42-44
Memory Verse: _____
Notes: _____

Week 16: Psalms 45-47
Memory Verse: _____
Notes: _____

Week 17: Psalms 48-50
Memory Verse: _____
Notes: _____

Week 18: Psalms 51-54
Memory Verse: _____
Notes: _____

Week 19: Psalms 55-57
Memory Verse: _____
Notes: _____

Week 20: Psalms 58-60
Memory Verse: _____
Notes: _____

Week 21: Psalms 61-63
Memory Verse: _____
Notes: _____

Week 22: Psalms 64-67
Memory Verse: _____
Notes: _____
_____

Week 23: Psalms 68-69
Memory Verse: _____
Notes: _____
_____

Week 24: Psalms 70-72
Memory Verse: _____
Notes: _____
_____

Week 25: Psalms 73-75
Memory Verse: _____
Notes: _____
_____

Week 26: Psalms 76-78
Memory Verse: _____
Notes: _____
_____

Week 27: Psalms 79-81
Memory Verse: _____
Notes: _____
_____

Week 28: Psalms 82-85
Memory Verse: _____
Notes: _____
_____

Week 29: Psalms 86-89
Memory Verse: _____

Notes:

Week 30: Psalms 90-92
Memory Verse:
Notes:

Week 31: Psalms 93-95
Memory Verse:
Notes:

Week 32: Psalms 96-99
Memory Verse:
Notes:

Week 33: Psalms 100-103
Memory Verse:
Notes:

Week 34: Psalms 104-105
Memory Verse:
Notes:

Week 35: Psalms 106
Memory Verse:
Notes:

Week 36: Psalms 107-108
Memory Verse:

Notes:_____

Week 37: Psalms 109-112
Memory Verse: _____
Notes:_____

Week 38: Psalms 113-116
Memory Verse: _____
Notes:_____

Week 39: Psalms 117-118
Memory Verse: _____
Notes:_____

Week 40: Psalms 119
Memory Verse: _____
Notes:_____

Week 41: Psalms 120-123
Memory Verse: _____
Notes:_____

Week 42: Psalms 124-127
Memory Verse: _____
Notes:_____

Week 43: Psalms 128-131
Memory Verse: _____
Notes:_____

Week 44: Psalms 132-134
Memory Verse: _____
Notes: _____

Week 45: Psalms 135-136
Memory Verse: _____
Notes: _____

Week 46: Psalms 137-139
Memory Verse: _____
Notes: _____

Week 47: Psalms 140-142
Memory Verse: _____
Notes: _____

Week 48: Psalms 143-145
Memory Verse: _____
Notes: _____

Week 49: Psalms 146-147
Memory Verse: _____
Notes: _____

Week 50: Psalms 148-150
Memory Verse: _____
Notes: _____

Made in the USA
Coppell, TX
10 June 2021

57209988R00081